On a Personal Note –

Specialized Poetry for All Occasions

Dorothell W. Muldrow

Kingdom Builders Publications LLC

© 2019 Dorothell W. Muldrow
On a Personal Note – Specialized Poetry for All Occasions
Kingdom Builders Publications, LLC

All rights reserved. No part of this book may be reproduced or transmitted in any form or by any means without written permission from the author.

Printed in the USA

ISBN 978-0-578-45299-9 Soft Cover
ISBN 237-0-000-66040-4 Hard Cover

Library of Congress Control Number 2019932271

Authored by
Dorothell W. Muldrow

Editor
Kingdom Builders Publications

Cover Design
LoMar Designs

DEDICATION

I dedicate this memoir to my dear husband, Reuben Delean Muldrow of 52 years, and our four children: Lisa, Mark, Ingell, and Anthony.

Likewise, I dedicate this first of many books to my God and Creator. He has called me to bring restoration through His word and through a special gift of poetry and song. Thank you all for your love and patience.

TABLE OF CONTENTS

DEDICATION iii
Introduction ix
Lord, I Hear You xi
Section One xii
  An Appreciation Poem for June Waters-Barnes 13
  Appreciation Poem for Mrs. Gilmore.. 14
  Appreciation Poem for Mickey - Maxine H. Garland 15
  Appreciation Poem for Margaret Sawyer 16
  Appreciation Poem for DeAnn 17
  Lady DeAnn 19
  Poem for an Excellent Director (Anita) 20
  Mr. & Mrs. Lonnie Ward - An Extraordinary Couple 22
  Poem of Daniel's Courage and of Might...................................... 24
  Conclusion: Daniel's Plight 25
  Appreciation Poem for Dr. Reginald Bolick................................ 26
  Appreciation Poem for Dr. Edward B. O'Dell 28
  Appreciation Poem for Jane and Her Group 30
  Appreciation Poem for Kevin & Joan 31
  Poem for Kim and Her Family 32
  Poem for "Lady Di" (Wonderful Music of Choice) 33
  Poem for Lisa Bruce... 35
  Poem for Lurline Jerry 36
  Poem for McIver and Willie Lee – An Extraordinary Couple . 37
  Poem for Milton and Allison 39
  Poem for Mrs. Lillie Mae Johnson 41
  Poem for Mrs. Mary Moses 42
  Pastor Bromell "Governance of the Baptist Church"............... 43
  Appreciation Poem for Rosa... 45
  Poem for Rozee and Vince... 46
  Poem for Syria... 47
  Poem for the Newsome's -When God Speaks 48
  Poem for Tonya 50
  Poem for Torrena 52
  Poem for Trey 54
  Poem for Brenda Goodson – A Brilliant Secretary 56

On a Personal Note – Specialized Poetry for All Occasions

Appreciation Poem to Franklin 57
Poem to Keith 58
Appreciation Poem for Renee' 60
Appreciation Poem for Carey and Joanne 62
Appreciation Poem for a Brilliant Salesperson, Carla 63
Appreciation Poem for Annie 65
Appreciation Poem for Cheryl 66
Appreciation Poem for Doris and Stenetta Johnson 68
Appreciation Poem to Dr. Paramore and Staff 70
Appreciation Poem for Jacqueline 71
Appreciation Poem for Lanelle 72
Appreciation Poem for Nancy Gordon 74
Appreciation Poem to Rebecca 76
Appreciation Poem for Tywan Goodson 78
Poem for Dr. Ray Willis - "The Healing Hands" 79
Mrs. Dennis, Lady of Enduring Faith 80
My Teacher Friend, Betsy Bird 81
The Pee Dee Baptist Association of Christian Education 82
Section Two 84
  Equip(meant) to be: A Poem for Anthony 85
  A Poem for My Daughter Ingell 87
  A Poem for My Oldest Son Mark 88
Section Three 90
  A Poem for My Granddaughter Anthonae 91
  A Poem for My Granddaughter McKenzie 94
  A Poem for My Granddaughter Jordan 96
Section Four 99
  A Poem for our Pastor's Anniversary 2018 100
  An Anniversary Poem for Charles and Lamar 101
Section Five 102
  A Poem to My Birthday (Sake) Barb Thayer 103
  A Birthday Poem for Kim 104
  A Poem for Marquis, Celebrating His 50th Birthday 105
  A Birthday Poem for Teresa 106
  An 80th Birthday Poem for Deacon Jerome Goodson 107
  Annette's Birthday Poem 109
  Celebrating One More Year of a Beautiful Life 110
  A Birthday and Appreciation Poem for A Special Teacher/

- Friend 111
- A poem for Betty's 65th Birthday Celebration 113
- A Birthday Poem for Bertha "PC" 114
- A Birthday Poem for "Pat" 116
- A Birthday poem For Braxton 117
- A Birthday Poem for Carrie 118
- A Poem for my Brother-In-Law Clarence for His 80th Birthday Celebration 119
- A Birthday Poem for Mae Alice 120
- A Birthday Poem for Mrs. Herlina D. Morris 122
- A Birthday poem for Sadie - a Longtime Friend 124
- An Appreciation and 80th Birthday Poem for Our Pastor..... 126
- A Welcome Poem for the Class Of `66 129
- Departing Poem for The Class Of `66 130
- A Poem for Arcola 131

Section Seven 133
- A Get well Poem for Nancy 134
- A Poem for Alphonso and Theola Of God's Fate 136
- A Poem for Edell – A Lady of Faith 137
- A Poem for Martha Ann – Courageous Lady of Choice 138
- Betsy's Plight 139
- A Poem for Murray 140

Section Eight 141
- The Enjoyable Road Trip 142

Section Nine 145
- A Poem to Barbara 146
- A Poem for Betty - A Friend and Sister in Christ 148
- A Poem for Beulah 149
- A Poem for Coach Walker 150
- How does your Garden grow? 152
- A Poem for Edith 153
- A Poem for Henrietta 154
- A Special Poem for the Installation Services 155
- Pen of A Ready Writer Society 156
- This Lady Pert 158
- Seeing Our Pastor through the Eyes of His Ministers 159
- Sunday Dinner at Mrs. Sarah's 161
- The Joy of Giving 162

On a Personal Note – Specialized Poetry for All Occasions

The Plight of Deidre' 163
The Right Touch Catering 164
Evans Family Chiropractic and Wellness 166
To Gloria - Our Esteemed Mayor 167
A Poem for Carolyn 169

Section Ten 171
  Barbara James - A Light for A Dark World 172
  A Poem for Joyce & AB of God's Grace Bestowed 173
  A Poem for Mr. & Mrs. Greene 175
  A Poem for Kyle Sherrod 176
  A Poem for Shaylah 177

Section Eleven 178
  A Poem for Alyssa 179
  A Poem of Grateful Thanks to Hattie 180
  A Poem for Margaret 181
  A Poem of Thankfulness to Kenneth 183
  A Poem of Thanks To Louise and Linton 184
  A Thank You Poem for Mrs. Gwen 185
  A Thank you Poem For you, Talaya 186
  A Thank You Poem to The Newsomes 187
  Mr. Giles, The Mailman and Servitor of Choice 189

Section Twelve 190
  A Poem for Your Wedding Day 191
  A Poem of Wedded Celebration to A Loving Couple 192
  A Wedding Poem for Kerwin & Annette 194
  A Poem for Timothy & Nyeshea On Your Wedding Day 196
  Because We Said, "I Do" 197
  Heaven Sent Two 198

Section Thirteen 199
  A Graduation Poem for our Granddaughter Cassie 200
  A Graduation Poem for Angelica 201
  A Graduation Poem for Christopher 202
  A Graduation Poem of Celebration for Deidrell 203
  A Graduation Poem for Kendric Dwayne 204
  A Graduation Poem for Kenyetta Nicole 206
  A Graduation Poem for My Granddaughter Nahla 208
  A Graduation Poem for Shameek 209
  A Poem for Jacquard 210

A Graduation Poem for Shalik Brown 211
Christine's Home of Her Own 213
Rushaun Muldrow Home of His Own 214
A House Warming Poem for Debra Hudson 215
A Graduation Poem for Nicholas 216
A Poem for George 217
A Congratulation Poem for Rev. Antwaun Richardson 218
Section Fourteen 220
A Poem for Emanuel James Dobson's Initial Sermon 221
Acknowledgments 222
About The Author 224

INTRODUCTION

I will introduce this personalized poem how God envisioned this book should be:

The first poem of this book is about how God envisioned me,
To embrace so many things that I personally see.
It can be about a person, place, or thing,
It will paint a picture, and what joy it will bring.

It is to spur the gift that I notice in sight,
I put it into words of a pleasant light.
The poems are to kindle hearts, and to bring a smile, warmly,
It will bring recognition of the person, and how others may see them normally.

The poems may make you smile, sometimes they may cause a joyful tear,
Most of all to share a gift to those who are very dear.
This is how God is using me,
To bring enjoyment and glee to those I see.

Dorothell Muldrow

The poems are friendly and to the point. The people in the poems have been perceived with a special effort of things that I sense of their character and mind. This is by the divine order of God. I have detected, discerned, observed, noticed, and have seen many things about each person. The poems are a way to comment and to bring a joyous response in return. You will see poems for birthday celebrations, graduations, appreciations, weddings, home-goings, get well, encouragement, and recognitions. Each poem is somewhat different. Each one has its own personal whelm.

The poems will bring how the innermost part of the celebrated has been exposed to be gratified as in knowing, "someone is in observance of you." Not for bad, but for good measure. There are so many people that have gifts or talents that they don't realize they have. Sometimes they are doing good things that no one else would take the time to do. These things go unnoticed. Sometimes it takes others to stir up the gift to bring them to view, then they recognize that they are doing more than they thought they could do.

Some may make you shed a tear; some will bring joy and a smile,
Some will bring great interest, and some you will see the extra mile.
You have a great variety to keep you on your heels,
Each poem will bring something different, and some with great ideals.

For the most part, it is introducing a person's story in a poem, and it is a written communication directed to another. Enjoy!!

On a Personal Note – Specialized Poetry for All Occasions

LORD, I HEAR YOU

*This is how I know God is near…He speaks softly in my ear.
"To declare your loving kindness in the morning, and your faithfulness every night."* (**Psalm 92:2**)

Lord, I hear the melodies and lyrics so sweetly in my ear,
The words and music, even the sweet aroma let me know you are near.
Lord, I hear you~ Lord, I feel you~ now I know you,
Help me use this gift through songs and lyrics so true.

I feel your touch in the mornings before I rise,
It wakes me up from my sleep, that I know is very wise.
It is either by your touch, your voice, or by a ring,
I am always listening for what it will bring.

Sometimes it brings a song~ sometimes it brings a word,
Sometimes it brings a warning which I know is preferred.
That's how you speak to me, because I have an ear,
To hear what the spirit is saying that you are near.

You always get my attention, because you want to hear from me,
I need that quiet time with you Lord, so you can show me what I should be.
You drop things in my spirit that paints a picture so true,
I make it poetic and it captures whatever one do.
It is a gift from you, indeed I know that's true,
Because you guide my hand and help with the writing too.

Thank you, God.

Dorothell Muldrow

Section One

Appreciation

AN APPRECIATION POEM FOR JUNE WATERS-BARNES

A good name is more desirable than great riches; to be esteemed is better than silver or gold. **(Proverbs 22:1)**

June, *a special lady of uniqueness* that I've known for a while,
We have a friendship that never waver, and always shows genuineness with a smile.
We've worked many hours together, and it was such a pleasure working with you.
The job had its ups and downs, but we trusted God and we made it through.

We have a special friendship, that we kept over the years,
We enjoyed the "Women's Retreat," which brought enjoyment and happy tears.
June, I thank you for your kindness and thoughtfulness too,
For staying in touch over the years and bringing others to the retreat with you.
I am including you in my poem book to be an item to enjoy along with the others,
It will be an enjoyment and encouragement to our sisters and our brothers.

Blessings to you, June.

Dorothell Muldrow

APPRECIATION POEM FOR MRS. GILMORE

A Songster in Christ the Savior

I shall sing always of the loving deeds of the Lord; throughout every generation I shall proclaim your faithfulness. **(Psalm 89:1)**

A poem for you Mrs. Gilmore, for God's call through you,
To use your voice so dearly, to bring restoration and to renew.
Your melodious voice and the gift through it you bring,
None other but God could plant such a beautiful thing.

You have blessed so many across the years,
Using the gift of song to be sweet music to the ears.
What a unique voice, and so naturally done,
You do it God's way knowing the Holy Spirit has won.

So in observation of you, I want to give a flower so true,
To be written in poetry, that is what God had me do.
I hope that you've saved some of your songs as to keep,
So folks can continue hearing the gift of specialty so deep.
Your choir has always been special, and the selection of songs are so great,
God bless your musician, she enhances them and relate.

She knows her special gift, and she carries it especially well,
Salem has something golden, and it more than I can tell.
God bless your new edifice, that He has truly provided,
You were patient and you waited, knowing His work and Spirit is invited.
There will be beauty inside, as it is on the outside,
Remember God as the builder, and He is also in the inside.
God's blessings upon you all.

APPRECIATION POEM FOR MICKEY – MAXINE H. GARLAND

Mickey, you are someone special, whom I've found to be so true;
Vernon, a true friend across the street, watches out for you.
Oh what frog collection, and the flower garden too;
I see much treasures all around, where fond memories accrue.

Mickey, so many birds and squirrels to watch, from your glass porch and favorite chair;
It gives you consolation, to know that God is near.
Mickey, you feed your birds daily, as God grant you the pace;
The squirrels have their fun too, as they run, eat, and race.

Your backyard draws much activity, with the birds and their neighboring friends;
It also brings much joy to watch, their play as each day ends.
It is so nice knowing you; it brings joy to my heart,
Just know I won't forget you Mickey, and I knew that from the start.

Thank you for the time I spent; and the things I were able to do.
Everything is for a season, I'm so glad it was with you.

Dorothell Muldrow

APPRECIATION POEM FOR MARGARET SAWYER

(Being Herself)

It gives me great pleasure, to do this poem for you,
To say those things that I see so kind, and so very true.
You are always so giving; in your manner and your way,
Having the right character; in all the things you say.

You make me smile; with your vim and wit,
It cheers my heart, like a light that is lit.
You say I encourage you, but you also encourage yourself,
There's so much that you give; not to hold, or to put on a shelf.

I enjoy our inspired talks, about our God and King,
Which is above all troubles, of whatsoever, and everything.
Thank you for being my Christian friend, to strengthen each other's mind,
The Lord knows what we need, someone to share, and to be kind.

If you wonder if your gift is…going the extra mile,
Just know yours is to cheer, and to make someone smile.
Keep on being yourself, singing the Songs of Zion utmost,
"Giving Honor" to the Father, to the Son, and to the Holy Ghost.

It was a pleasure writing this poem, gathering things to say about you,
God bless you "Marg," and may all your dreams come true.

APPRECIATION POEM FOR DEANN

Hi, my encourager and confidante friend, so helpful to my listening ear,
You've soothed my aching spirit; of the many things I could not bear.
You help me to understand, when things had gone so wrong,
Helping me to know that God is working and is directing it all along.

He got my attention and even gave me something to do,
You see, I'm writing poems and more poems, to encourage and to keep me from being blue.
My special songs are in holding, waiting for its special day,
I let God order my steps my friend, He will let me know what's on the way.

DeAnn, it's been quite a journey, oh, how rugged it has been,
I know that God is with me, and He's just working my "thick and thin."
DeAnn, I appreciate you so much, and all you've done in helping me,
I could not have made it, had you not encouraged me to see.

To see how God was building me, for this task to take on,
I still can't see what's in the midst; I'll have to wait until it's done.
You are my genuine encourager, God placed you in my path,
The Lord knows our every longing, and we know what He hath.

Dorothell Muldrow

I look forward to sharing with you, the work that I have done,
Just to share it, and to say God's in it, and that the battle is won.
I thank God for the ability of writing these lovely poems,
It certainly has cheered many hearts, and it keeps me scribbling the norms.

A poem for you DeAnn, a picture which proves so true.

LADY DEANN

What a vessel! What a vessel!
In God's vineyard, He trust;
You have helped so many people,
For direction, as you must.

God's given you a special gift,
To console, and to restore;
Those souls that's been captivated,
By the whelms of things untold.

God bless you Lady DeAnn,
For the things you say and do;
It will hold true to the end,
With faith and hope in you.

Just a few lines to describe,
The gift I see in you;
God's gift of restitution,
Of the loss, the oppressed, and the blue.

God bless your ministry,
And all the things you'll do;
With God all things are possible,
With His power and Glory too.

Dorothell Muldrow

POEM FOR AN EXCELLENT DIRECTOR (ANITA)

Just a poem of appreciation, of all you've done for me,
Speaking of the beautiful occasion, of our Renewal Agree.
I will always be thankful of how God kept us through the years,
He brought us to such a special time in our life; some joy, some tears.

Anita, I am still reminiscing of how well things went,
And all the many ideas you put forth for this event.
Preplanning the Renewal, certainly took some work,
But, you and Ingell…your work you did not shirk.

There were so many compliments about how unique it was,
We had God on our side, so no way it could pause.
It flowed so lovely, with just what we had in place,
Great minds work together; not a negative, not a trace.

Every little piece that was used and suggested,
Fell right into place; even the people, so blessed.
The spirit knows the spirit, and knew what things needed to be.
Only one thing was done, and it was obvious to see.

It brought about laughter, during the Renewal Vow,
This little oops brought a smile, and we worked it out somehow.
God had it in control,
And we saw the hidden agenda, of the super natural unfold.

Just remembering back when I wanted to help in some way,
You told me to sit to the side, "I got it, okay?"
I was still wondering, had I miss some instructions somehow,
So I ask the question, Ingell answered, "There's nothing right now."

"Just flowing right along," she said.
"Keeping things afloat and staying ahead."
Everything was so beautiful, just as God planned,
With special things in place, I couldn't complain.

Thank you again Anita, for a job well done,
You took care of matters really good, we even had fun.

Blessings to you, victory has been done.

MR. & MRS. LONNIE WARD – AN EXTRAORDINARY COUPLE

Mr. and Mrs. Ward, a couple that stands out,
You are winners in progress; you know what that's all about.
You have met the inevitable, straight forward hand in hand,
Only the Good Lord, as you met the demand.

I've known you over the years, special people in every way,
Always were open to others in the gatherings you display.
Hand in hand, side by side, courageously in faith you trod,
Can't think of anyone so unique, you were handmade by God.

Including you in my poem book that God envisioned for me,
Of many gifts to pass on to others, embracing the things I observe and see.
We miss you from the couple's ministry, which you fitted in so well,
You brought many highlights, to enhance it to excel.

We thought to give it up, and let someone else have a chance,
But so far, we are sticking with it; and God has envisioned it to advance.
Our couples do presentations and it has gone very well,
We plan to have a couples' workshop, with information that we can tell.

We think of you often, and what vigor and might you embrace,
It gives us more gumption to stand, and to keep on running this race.
We always enjoy our visit, when we get chance to come by,
We enjoy the laughter and fellowship, which is mutual, we can't deny.

The children have sheltered you in their home, and are taking good care of you,
With no regrets, all love God see's it all, and the blessings are in view.
We will keep you both in prayer, and please do the same for us,
We are all fighters for the kingdom, it's not easy, but we do as we must.
God's continued blessings upon you,

God loves you, and we do too.

Dorothell Muldrow

POEM OF DANIEL'S COURAGE AND OF MIGHT

To my brother Daniel, who've crossed the many miles,
To come back to see family, which have brought many smiles.
Oh how good to see you brother, of so many years apart,
God fulfill my every longing, because this was dear to my heart.

The Lord knows the things that we need, and he fills them, if we just keep still,
He knew about my longing to see you my brother, and to make it happen at will.
He knows about the time we'd lost, it has now past and gone,
I also know God redeems the time, it was already there before we were born.

It is so Awesome, how God answered my prayer,
He knows our every weakness and brought us joy to share.
Can you imagine, if this day had not happened, of all the hidden things,
Now we can rejoice of this discovery and use God's gifts He brings.

Thank you, my brother, for making this dream come true,
God did an act in you, and He allowed it to come through.
And I thank my Heavenly Father, for bringing you back, "You were due."

I'm so glad you bit the hook, and took off and made the drive,
All the way from Arizona, with God keeping you alive.
Oh what courage it took, oh what faith by the book,
God is the only one; all it takes is just one look.
A look at the Savior, and trust Him and believe,
He will never, never forsake you, nor ever will He leave.

Thank you, my brother Daniel, we have catching up to do,
We can't do it all in one visit, but God will make it happen for sure.

You know the way now brother, God made it plain to see,
Give it much thought my brother, it is meant to be.
Thank you God, for my answered prayer; you have blessed me so true,
You gave me back my brother, and his life you gave back too.

CONCLUSION: DANIEL'S PLIGHT

You told me about Vietnam, you told me about the struggle there,
You told me about how you made it back,
Not knowing how or when you returned home here.

You came through the post-traumatic depression, God amend those things quiet well,
So glad you are among the living, only God's record can tell.
So glad we are together, it's been a long, long time,
I thank God for His timing, to bring this reunion sublime

I love you my brother, your sister Dot

Dorothell Muldrow

APPRECIATION POEM FOR DR. REGINALD BOLICK
An Esteemed Doctor of Choice

Dr. Bolick, you are the esteemed doctor, who have crossed the many miles,
By your surgical expertise that brought many smiles.
You have met a great milestone of much gratitude,
We all can't thank you enough, for your kindness and services you did without an attitude.

Oh! the number of procedures, you did through your anointed hands,
You were an answered prayer for many patients by God's commands.
I remember when you first came aboard, a few years before I came along,
You joined up with the Houck Group, later, the partnership became strong.
Others were added, and it gave the practice a new song.

You became so popular, your expertise spoke for you,
Sewing and mending the innermost being, then increase in number grew.
It was such a privilege to work in your room,
I for sure knew my day would be good without any gloom.
When I was very new, you gave me much confidence,
You made me feel I would make it even through offense.

Excellency! A job well done, when all wounds were closed,
Healing did take place during the recuperation period, all because of what was exposed.
Your hands were special instruments, that God used in His plan,

On a Personal Note – Specialized Poetry for All Occasions

You can rest assure and have no doubt, you did a great work by His command.
Enjoy your retirement, take it in stride,
Relax, be spoiled, take it easy, enjoy the ride.
I thought about what you said about your hearing, eyes, and your hands,
God is just saying, "Be still and know that I am God" you've met all my demands.
Dr. Bolick, I truly enjoyed writing this poem for you,
I hope I'd painted a picture of the esteemed person that I knew.

Dorothell Muldrow

APPRECIATION POEM FOR DR. EDWARD B. O'DELL

God has given me a gift of writing of people and things~
that has touched my life in some special way;
I spent much time meditating in the quietness of the mornings,
then God gives me what I need to say.

Dr. O'Dell, I am establishing a personalized poem book,
Which I plan to have published one day,
You will be able to take a look at my work,
that will soon come, I'll say.

Just remembering people and things…you came to my mind,
Remembering you sent a good word up for me, which was so very kind.
I know you are surprised to receive this magnificent gift,
Seeing you on the billboard gave my memory a lift.

So, I wanted to remember you with something, while you live,
My gift to you in poem, this is what I'll give.
We both are getting older, and have crossed many of miles,
God has been good to us ~though some tears~ but there still were many smiles.

I will name my book, On a Personal Note,"
These poems paint a picture of things I have observed, and those that gave support.
Dr. O'Dell, you believed in me and my work,
You had confidence knowing my work I would not shirk.

I am glad for the 29 1/2 years spent in the O.R., there were so much to do and see;
The encouragement you gave, was strengthening and a wonderful

key.
I did finish that race, as Paul would say **(2 Timothy 4:7)**,
I met retirement on one special day.

Life is good, and I am doing just fine,
I am working through many things, because of believing in the divine.
Just a few words to say, I thought about you,
For being such a good doctor, and the work that you do.

Blessings to all your employed family and home family too.

APPRECIATION POEM FOR JANE AND HER GROUP

An appreciation poem for you, Mrs. Jane,
Of one who goes the extra mile, and not look for gain.
It certainly was a pleasure to join with all of you,
To all the events you've invited us to, and with hospitality so true.

It is so good to have unity in all you set out to do,
Reaching out and loving one another and seeing God's love come bursting through.
Jane you are special, I saw it from the start,
So caring and warm-hearted, and always doing your part.

We really liked our bus ride, being with you all was lots of fun,
Both bus drivers drove very well, and they got the job done.
Safely there and back, we had no doubt,
We put God on the steering wheel; now that is, what it's all about.

Thank you once again for including us to go along,
Next time when we ride together, let us all sing a song.

APPRECIATION POEM FOR KEVIN & JOAN

The Couple of Choice

Here's to you Kevin and Joan, the couple that I see and observed,
You are that couple that meet the challenges of a long life in reserve.
The vows that you made to each other has been actively used,
Each time that I see you together, it appears never abused.

God says to carry one another's burdens, with caring and with much thought,
No need to worry about you two, you are doing what God taught.
You support each other so dearly, being sure each other's feet are on ground,
What a special couple I see you are, what a built foundation you've found.

Keep being a good example, being content as you are,
God does not fall short of His word and hasn't left you so far.
God bless you Kevin and Joan of my words to you,
Just continue being the couple you are, being steadfast and true.

This is a gift God gave me through the journey I've been through,
To share and to encourage others, so please keep up what you do.
Oh yes, I have a story too, I get teary eyes of joy as I think of it,
Through my experience, God refined me, which I don't regret one bit.

Dorothell Muldrow

POEM FOR KIM AND HER FAMILY

I thought to write a poem of a unique and special friend,
It's about you, Kim and Brice, also Kathryn, Hampton, and baby Bowen;
This beautiful plight of interest, where God took the lead,
Starting with the special guy you met, that led to a wedded deed.

Then you got to know each other, as this man of God's great choice;
Then later, God decided to bless you with a business, and you being the boss.
You have made much progress, as in the family way,
God blessed you with girl/boy twins, and then came baby Bowen one day.

Brice is right by your side, partnering in the business right well,
Two is better than one, and with God, three makes it swell.

You found an adorable home, which God has entrusted to you,
With a lovely white fence around it, and such a beautiful view.
God bless you and your family, as you let Him guide your way,
Being wise and confident is a must, and always remember to pray.

What an adorable family, "Every good and perfect gift is from above."
(James 1:17)

The children are so lovely, and you both are embracing God's love.

POEM FOR "LADY DI" (WONDERFUL MUSIC OF CHOICE)

for Diana Williamson Pauley for sharing her God given gift of music in voice and musical song

A poem for you "Lady Di," for the person I see you are,
You're that light I see in the corner that shines afar.
Some may see it, and to some it's farfetched,
They've missed it somehow, blinded by their own little niche.

There's richness in your music, and you've used it with all your might,
Each season that God put you in, you work to make it right.
Sometimes we have to stand, sometimes we have to move,
And sometimes God carry you to a new height, that only He will approve.

God has given me the gift of poetry, to cheer and to plant a seed,
Whomever He drops in my spirit, I take ownership of it, and then proceed.
I cheer, I encourage, I point out what I see in each individual one,
To bring about the light of God, so they may know what God has done.

Just remember "Lady Di," your season does move on,
God will never belittle it, however trivial, but His work will get done.
When God gave you your new job, it was an open spring,
He started a new work in you there, and oh what joy did it bring.

God sees the big picture, and He knows all that goes on,
Keep your wits about you, the battle has already been won.
I say again, I cheer, I encourage, only God can truly guide,

Dorothell Muldrow

I can only plant the seed, as we humbly abide.

I enjoyed writing this poem for you, I will miss your gift of music so much,
You brought something special to us, to me, it was like the *Midas Touch*.

The enemy comes to kill and to destroy, and he also comes to steal,
But God has the greatest power, just you stand and be real.
Music is the soul's own speech,
For heights and the depths no words can reach,
Blessings to you "Lady Di," wherever your endeavors teach.

POEM FOR LISA BRUCE
A Special Friend, and Servitor of Choice

Lisa, you are that person, that for years you've been by my side,
I don't really have to see you, but I know you are there if I need a guide.
You have stuck with the duty, of keeping the Nursery,
It shows commitment and endurance but being faithful is the key.

You are a person that can be counted on, in whatever you set out to do,
Very dependable with that great smile of yours, which can win others to be helpful too (smile).
You are also diligent in your work ethics, I know because I worked with you,
Can't find a better person that will work with you, and with great effort too.

It is good to know you Lisa, you've been a true and special friend,
I look forward to my hug on Sunday mornings, it is real, and you don't pretend.
It's been a pleasure to do this poem for you, giving a little flower while you live,
These are things I like doing to touch a heart and be willing to give.

Just remember real friendships are rare,
We have that special invisible one, that is always near.

Blessings to you, Lisa.

Dorothell Muldrow

POEM FOR LURLINE JERRY
A Brilliant Social Worker and Servitor of Choice

Lurline, Lurline! I have some words for you,
To describe a person of diligence, caring, and true.
It's you, that have so much to give, through your words and your deeds,
You meet the things on the job and meet the community needs.

Don't see how you do it, I know you count on God's strength to provide,
He's always the one you depend upon, for the need and for His guide.
The food program is going well, you are handling it really good,
You have willing people to help, that's a plus, and they should.

You are meeting the needs of the community, which I know God is very pleased,
I know when you do this great deed, it sets your heart at ease.
I love hearing you speak, you have a gift so true,
You make me smile and feel good inside, and others enjoy it too.

Continue in your work, and keep sharing in your talk,
You will leave your mark in society, by your good mannerisms and walk.
Just a little poem for you, to give a flower along the way,
Keep on doing what you do, a great reward God has for you one day.

Blessings to you, Lurline.

POEM FOR MCIVER AND WILLIE LEE – AN EXTRAORDINARY COUPLE

McIver and Willie Lee

You are the couple that is surely inspired by God's speed,
You move by His direction, allowing Him to lead.
Your lives have been planted by sticking to life's highs and lows,
You have been blessed by waiting, knowing that God only knows.

You moved at God's speed as you both were being planted,
There have been so many things along the way that has been granted.
You both are committed to what you set out to do,
And you do it together, from what I can see, has proved to be true.
Your children have been spurred up in their potentialities,
Oh, how proud to see them working with their capabilities.

I love it when you sing, "It was a great thing that He did for me,"
Not only does it touch my heart, it touches others to realize to see;
Of what Jesus did for all of us, hanging from the rugged cross,
Oh what a great thing He did, so our souls would not be loss.

You sing the song with gumption, as though you know what you're singing about,
No one can carry it like you two, you both are "winners," and that's no doubt.
The strength of the family is what God is looking for,
With God backing it, you can't ask for anything more.
Keep up the good work, realizing that it's not easy all the time,
Prayer is the key and won't cost you one dime.
We aren't perfect in all we thrive to do,
We just keep looking up, and God gets us through.

Dorothell Muldrow

Just another poem to share what God can do,
He does this through others, including you two.
Don't be dismayed, you are walking in view,
Of the Savior, the world has need of you.

Thank you, McIver and Willie Lee, for being the extraordinary couple in so many ways.

On a Personal Note – Specialized Poetry for All Occasions

POEM FOR MILTON AND ALLISON
Unique Couple of Choice

Milton and Allison, two people that are special,
You have a gift of distinction, that is very essential.
I love your leadership, and you both are our friends;
So glad to have you in our stead, you deal greatly with the trends.

You both shuffle the hours, between home, things, and family,
You get it done all the time, and it's done so faithfully.
We certainly appreciate you and all you help us do;
Couldn't ask for a better couple to count on, and to be around too.

Just so you know you have been observed, not only by us you see,
Be mindful of what vessels you are, and what God have you be.
Allison, you remind me of a flower garden, that is maintained very well,
You cover the ground with many ideas, more than any of us can tell.

Milton comes along and water the ground, by filling in those spots with plenty,
Making sure there's nothing unturned and filling what's empty (my parable).
Talking about life things and how we shuffle them along;
Asking God for more strength so they won't go wrong.

I thank God for you two, to us you are our special friends,
We are glad we can count on you and know the goodness God sends.
God sends those people that fit to be ideal,
To help in times of need, and to be genuinely real.

Dorothell Muldrow

That's who you are, the couple of choice,
We don't have to look to any other source.
That's a great thing you see, just keep doing what you do,
Counting on the Divine, He'll always have work for you.

POEM FOR MRS. LILLIE MAE JOHNSON

The Lady of Durability Plus

Mrs. Johnson, this is a poem I've written for you,
Because in observation, I've seen the strength you have so true.
I've known you over the years of your dedication to your church and work,
Being dependable and having the expertise of the needs, you do not shirk.

Some call you "Lillie Mae," some call you "Mrs. Johnson,"
Dr. Wilson and the team called you, "Mae,"
And when they get to see you, they still call you that today.

Death came to a few of your loved ones, and you've been a strong tower for your family,
You challenged your hip surgery, and now have more stability.
That's the way God is, the mysteries of His ways,
He's been doing things like that since the Ancient of Days.

You are a courageous lady, in all that I see you do,
God has blessed you mightily, because of your trust in Him and sincerity too.
Mrs. Johnson, it has been great chatting about you,
Of a lovely lady of durability and much stamina that proves to be true.

I say durability, because you have witnessed and survived so much,
You don't look like what you've been through, and that's nothing but God's *Midas Touch*.
God bless you, Mrs. Johnson, as you continue throughout life's journey,
Keep looking up to Jesus, for He will make it worthwhile; like He does for so many.

Dorothell Muldrow

POEM FOR MRS. MARY MOSES

Mrs. Moses, you are one of God's gifts for exercising your voice,
To sing the songs of Zion, giving praise and to rejoice.
Folks have enjoyed your singing all through the many years,
Not only that, but seeing the Christ in you, even through the tears.

You raised your family, and God has given you so much,
You kept right on going forward, because you stayed in touch.
In touch with the Savior; knowing He's right by your side,
Keeping in mind why you are here, and why our Savior died.

You sing with such power, and you know where that came from,
He gave you the anointing, and all that you've become.
Keep singing the songs of Zion, bless those coming in and going out,
Continue being a blessing, that's what God's love is all about.

It gives me much pleasure, to do this poem for you,
I've truly enjoyed your singing, and to admire a lady so true.
Keep holding up the blood stained banner, continuing what you do,
While standing on His promises, more blessings will come through.

PASTOR BROMELL "GOVERNANCE OF THE BAPTIST CHURCH"

Pastor Cecil L. Bromell, M. Div.

To thank you very much from our class, Pastor Bromell,
For this week of knowledge that you taught very well.
You answered our questions of the things of great thought,
There was clarity in the answers that were brought.

It certainly cleared our minds, of the way we had believed,
Oh you gave us understanding, and we are grateful for what we received.
You talked about Daniel, being in the lions' den,
How God shut the lions' mouths; Daniel came out knowing God was within.
You talked about the three Hebrew boys, and how they withstood,
It was hot in that fiery furnace; God being number four
Controlled it, saved the boys, as only one could.
You mentioned Phillip and the Eunuch, how he embraced the Eunuch with the word,
It made me think of a member of my church that could not read,
But came to believe by what he heard.

You talked about Adam and the *"wo" man*, and how Eve was attached as flesh and bone,
It took a lil' work from the master, to make Adam a helpmate,
So he wouldn't be alone.
I like the part about saying, amen,
We must know the truth, before we can comprehend.
I know I will be cautious as I say it from now on,
We have to listen for the truth, then we can say well done.

You talked about many things, that we needed to know,
We are thankful for the knowledge, it will surely help us grow.

Dorothell Muldrow

God is a God of order you said, in the governance of the church,
We will continue to study to show ourselves approved, and keep on in the search.
Like God, you gave us more than enough
The abundance of knowledge has given so much.
We will leave so much better now, than whence we came,
Thank you again, Pastor Bromell, we now have a different aim.

APPRECIATION POEM FOR ROSA

This time has come for you to be at ease, and at rest;
God granted it to you, and surely, this is not a test.
Gird up your loins, sit back, and relax,
Just smile, breathe deep, hold it! Blow it out to the max.

Thirty years, it took much dedication, patience, and might;
We know if it had not been for the Lord on your side,
You could not have done that right.
Many family and friends are here; showing support and love today,
It is special, it is superb, and oh what joy we brought your way.

I brought to you this lovely poem, to cheer you and to say;
Happy Retirement Rosa! And enjoy your special day.

Enjoy this time in your life. God granted it to you. Take it in stride.

Dorothell Muldrow

POEM FOR ROZEE AND VINCE

A poem written to say to the two of you,
You have a love that is tailored made and so very true.
You've been together now for a number of years,
Through sickness, through health, and some joyous tears.

Then you found strength, through the highs and lows,
You've combatted this world's turmoil, and in you it shows.

I'm proud of the way you both hold on,
What God has put together, you will never be alone.
He will always be by your side, whatever comes your way,
He's proved that to you many times, each and every day.

This gathering today means so much to me,
Family, friends, and having God in the midst, makes three.
Rozee, you are my birthday sake, and my goddaughter too,
Each are unique, what a blessing to have both attached to you.

You have a family well-knitted together, which is very, very unique,
God made it all possible, and you didn't have to seek.
God's blessings this pre-New Year's Day and forever always!
We couldn't be in a better place, than with God's grace and love, and much PRAISE!

POEM FOR SYRIA

A Lovely Young Lady and Stylist of Choice

"She will place on your head an ornament of grace; A crown of glory she will deliver to you." **(Proverbs 4:9)**

Syria, to do a poem for you is such a delight,
Because the qualities I see in you has been brought to light.
You are a go-getter with a sensible direction in mind,
It seems you know what you want, in life with maturity so kind.

You will do well Syria, keeping Christ as your lead,
Don't fall for love too quickly, let the spirit guide that special need.
I've detected that you know the Savior, taught by your family tree,
I have discerned the warmness of heart, that you have entreated me.

You spoke about your Grandma Ollie Mae, and the things she instilled in you,
She's gone now, but not forgotten, and left a legacy that was passed on so true.
And now, your mom Detra, is in your stead for sure.

God blessed me when I met you, He knew I needed the care,
When he entrusted you to be my stylist, it has been excellency to every strand of hair.
Continue being that lovely young lady, with a character most people know,
You won't have to look over your shoulder, no matter wherever you go.

Dorothell Muldrow

POEM FOR THE NEWSOME'S –WHEN GOD SPEAKS

Sharing good news by the inspiration of God for Dr. Newsome and his wife Laura

You both fell in my spirit while meditating today,
I paused in spirit, and these are the words God gave me to say
The spirit led me of words on why you were led this way,
Strong desire, you said Laura, and because of it you are both here with us today.

I do know that you both are spirit led, and have the Word of God in hand,
God sent you this way at a time as this to give word on how to stand.
You are interested in the Church well-being, and you have good intentions too,
I do believe that this is one of the new things God is doing, because of your reasoning so true.

I've written this in the way of a poem, which is a gift God has given me,
He always gives me what to say, and He is writing it to a certain degree.
To me it's sending a message to someone He wants to reach,
All I know it is awesome, and it is another way to teach.

I was meditating in the spirit, and God met me there,
A sweet aroma past my nose, and I knew then God's spirit was near.

I asked verbally, "Could this be so?"
I felt something so real, I wouldn't let go.

On a Personal Note – Specialized Poetry for All Occasions

What mysteries of God's ways and how He will reveal;
This was something I didn't let go, because it felt so real.
It felt so strong of this answer, I thought my heart would drop,
I became so joyfully emotional, for that moment I couldn't even stop.
I want to pass this on to you, because this is what my spirit led me to do.
There is a reason why you both are here, only God knows, and will acknowledge it to you.

POEM FOR TONYA
Special Friend and Sister in Christ

It gives me great pleasure to do this poem for you,
Of someone who have proved to be trustworthy and true.
Tonya, I am still reminiscing, on our friendship dinner meet,
We had a wonderful time catching up on each other's plight; that we still have to complete.

It was so wonderful to see you, and learn of the progress you made,
You could not have made it without the "Good Lord's" aid.
You are good at shuffling the hours at hand, knowing God is your underfoot,
You prayed as you met the hours, an answered prayer stayed in route.

You are going to be successful, and your persevering will not be in vain,
The road has been rough my friend, but just wait to see what you will gain.
You believed in your home; you never gave up on it at all;
You tarried long in your waiting, but God had it all in His call.

Little by little, you will get it in order,
Day by day, and through the months; after a while, it won't be a bother.
It's been a pleasure having you as a confident friend,
You are young, and I am old; and it doesn't matter, nor does it offend.

We were always able to connect in our very thoughts,
There is a true spiritual bind, that I know our God exalts.
You shuffle the family care between work and other things,

On a Personal Note – Specialized Poetry for All Occasions

God is truly holding you up, with His power and strength He brings.

You have a good husband and mother, and the children have their own special gifts,
It's blessed, how you look after each other, even when obstacles are in the midst.
Tonya, keep doing what you do,
Trusting and believing, holding on and being true.

And everyone who has this hope in Him purifies himself, just as He is pure.
(1 John 3:3)

Dorothell Muldrow

POEM FOR TORRENA

For Your Unwavering Caring, and Sharing Your Gift of Hospitality

The greatest achievements are those that benefit others.
~Denis Waitley

I can easily write about you Torrena, because of the first impression in meeting you,
You were kind and had the chemistry, on how to treat a person brand new.
It was very cold in the area where we sat, and you were considerate of how I felt,
I was feeling so very cold; I surely needed a melt.

I will never forget the kindness shown,
It will be remembered on the list of special things I've known.
Thank you for the warmness to someone you never knew,
It was a God move, and the angels way in you.

You have an unwavering spirit, and it shows upon your face,
Not letting unexpecting things bother you, when they come into place.
You seem to trust your instinct, with life's challenges very well,
Some maybe a task at hand, but your aim is to win and to excel.

I learned of how you helped a friend in need, who was distraught and so blue,
One who did not have direction, not even a clue.
But you turned that around, just by the wisdom words that you shared,
You lent a hand when it was needed, and showed that you cared.

Thank you for your kindness, thank you for all the things you shared.
Just to include you in my poetry, special prose about you,
These are the words God inspired me to say,
And to bless you through them too.
May life for you be full, with the seeds you have sown,
May your returns be bountiful with what you have shown.

Dorothell Muldrow

POEM FOR TREY

An Employed Servitor of Choice

Be kindly affectionate to one another with brotherly love, in honor giving preference to one another; not lagging in diligence, fervent in spirit, serving the Lord.
(Romans 12:10-11 NKJV)

Stopping by the GNC store, I met a young man named Trey,
He works there as an employee, and he helped me so much that day.
I was bothered with my neck and blood pressure, and he asked could he pray for me?
Of course, I said, "Please do," and he did; and we both touched and agree.

He recommended a few good products, which to try out to see,
I left there that day, did not take any medicine, because the spirit had set me free.
He asked me did I know Jesus? I said, "Very well indeed,"
We started sharing our inspiring stories and how God will meet the need.

I left there that day to have the pre-admit testing done for my neck surgery.
Not knowing that my blood pressure would be in the normal range collectively.
All because of the prayer you prayed, Trey,
That rescued me that day.
I've had my surgery, and healing is taking place,
You prayed that God would be with me, and now minimal pain is upon my face.
It was so good you knew Jesus, the spirit connected right away,
Where two or three gathers in His name, He's sure to be there without delay.

On a Personal Note – Specialized Poetry for All Occasions

We talked about how God reveals things, through dreams and inspiration,
And how it takes obedience, to hear His voice of direction.

Thank you, Trey, for being that lamp that brighten my day,
That is how God uses us to help in some way.

Dorothell Muldrow

POEM FOR BRENDA GOODSON – A BRILLIANT SECRETARY
in Appreciation for Her Work Ethics

Brenda, I've written this poem about you, because I've observed some things so dear and true,
Which does not go unnoticed, of the work I see you do.
From paper to computer, to housekeeping and child care,
I don't know how you do it all, and always willing to share.

You take care of family, and some friends too,
You grab up so many children, teaching them what to do.
I can say your work speaks for you, and you do it with such ease,
You depend upon God only, because he holds all the keys.

Just a little poem for you, to say I appreciate you,
For the times you've helped me out, to do the things I could not do.
Deacon Jerome, your angel, God sent him to you,
He makes you a good husband, and prayer partner too.

I added his name to the poem, because he is a part of you,
He tolerates you being busy, in all the things you do.
Keep doing your very best, although trials and tests will come,
The things you don't get done, God will do them and then some.

I did not mention your garden, your plants and flowers of hue,
"God's Garden" I call it, will keep you close in view.
You can see Him in all His colors, he also sees you too,
Just keep doing what you do, because He is watching you.

APPRECIATION POEM TO FRANKLIN
A Salesman, Writer, Singer, and Servitor of Choice

It's been a pleasure meeting you Franklin, and the help you gave us too;
Our visit at the store was most rewarding, and my husband and I learned some things unique about you.
We came in for a purchase, and a conversation grew,
Didn't know you were a scholar of God; also, a writer and singer so true.

You shared your gift of writing, and some of your material too;
I'm taking good care of your notebook, it's in good hands like Allstate, prove to be true.
I am observant, and my first impression went over well,
You have a great salesmanship under your buckle, and I'm sure most people can tell.

Your customer service attitude is mapped all over you,
It's good that God is in it, His love is what's shining through.
Thank you, Franklin, for answering our questions, this poem is to appreciate you,
Now, I have to do something with my own writing, and to activate what's been long due.

The story lines in your songs have such reality and zeal,
It paints a vivid picture of their personality that's real.
I truly enjoy reading them, it gives me a smile as well,
I can see the hands of God in all of them; He's the helping hand, I can tell.

God bless you, Franklin, for all you are doing,
You are doing a great job with your gift, and we already know where that's going. (giving God the glory)

Dorothell Muldrow

POEM TO KEITH
A Servitor of Choice

Way to go! Keith. You've found your place in life.
You will help more and more children, and ready them for this world's strife.
When I read the article in the paper, I said, "My God knows who to choose,"
We need examples in society; God knows just who He can use.

This world is in a turmoil, and our future are our kids,
The record as I see it, has no holds bar, and not enough bids.
But I see you are making a difference, it gives an open view,
Everything that is being done right now, can change the picture to something brand new.

Just keep doing what you do, which is something good,
God is pleased with this project, keeping our children out of the hood.
You are making a difference in society, and we know you can't do it all,
Keith, the world needs more people like you, to prevent them from the fall.

A poem for you Keith, written from the spirit within,
To express what I see in you, and the help that God will send.
With my girl Ronnie by your side, she will keep you ever straight,

Always there to help all she can, she's a good wife and a wonderful helpmate.

On a Personal Note – Specialized Poetry for All Occasions

Keith, just take it day by day, letting God lead the way,
Some days are not going to be easy, it always helps when we pray.

Hey! I forgot about the picture in the paper, that is a good picture of you,
I see positiveness in your smile, and God is shining through it too.

Keep up the good work I say again, the world is in need of you.
I am so excited about what you are doing, keep your chin up, and always be true.

APPRECIATION POEM FOR RENEE'

Renee', I have no problem with writing this poem for you,
Because it will tell of someone I know, is especially true.
True to your word, true to yourself,
You give so much love and have plenty more left.

You shuffle your hours, doing your work by the bell,
You've been doing this for quite a while, managing very well.
You always handle your job, with optimism and might,
Being knowledgeable about what you do, getting the folks on flight.

We joined with you all on many occasions, and we followed your lead,
For you made great provisions, on what we would need.
Everything would always go smoothly, just as we expect it would,
You always know how to carry it out, as a duty should.

You have worked through situations, because of the prayers you'd prayed,
Your family is an example, with unity displayed.
Marvin, Joshua, and Karissa are your immediate family tree,
God has blessed you abundantly, because of the love and support you give humbly.
I think of your Mom and Dad, and the joy and cheer each brought,
Your Dad had so much wisdom, I'll always remember what he taught.
His aim was to set things in the right order, and he would not give up on it,
Until it was no longer a bother, he never would quit.
That was the kind of man he was, firm in his convictions,
Being as a strong tower for the family, not looking for any

recognitions.
Renee', you know you have some of your Daddy's wit, I can hear it in your talk,
All your siblings are cut from your Mom and Dad's pattern, I can see it in their walk.

I started out writing this poem, didn't know I had so much to say,
Just observing some things about you and the family, of joy and not dismay.
I enjoyed writing those things about your family tree,
Be grateful for the abiding love you all have, "God's love" is the key.

APPRECIATION POEM FOR CAREY AND JOANNE

Hear; for I will speak of excellent things; and the opening of my lips shall be right things. (Proverbs 8:6)

Oh! It gives me great pleasure to write about you,
A couple of distinction and pleasantness too.
"Jo," you do your poems and writings and you share them selflessly,
And Carey does his inspirational prayers and sing so heavenly.

Thank you both for allowing God to use you in such a mighty way,
It's not the amount of words you use, but what all you do and say.
Just a few words of expression of the things in observance of you,
Keep looking up, keep using your gifts, because God gave them for you to bless someone too.

Including you in my poem book to brighten up your day,
Joining in with all the others of what I've observed, and what God has me to say.

APPRECIATION POEM FOR A BRILLIANT SALESPERSON, CARLA

This is a poem for you Carla, to say I appreciate you,
When I walk into "Suit Expo," I see smiles with greetings too.
You manage your job well, and your boss knows that for sure,
You handle your customers so obsolete, keeping them happy and satisfied assure.

You certainly helped me in so many ways,
Being patient with me on those last-minute days.
You made sure of the sizes, right to the tee,
Even the color, which I didn't disagree.

Carla, you truly impress me, with your great Customer Service attitude,
Keep up the good work Carla, there are blessings God will include.
I cannot really thank you, for all that you have done,
I know you were only doing your job, we even had some fun.

Each time we come into the store, we appreciate you so much,
We always receive satisfaction, it's kind a like the *Midas Touch*.
You are so helpful to the customers, in managing what you do,
From using your measuring tape for sizing and helping them make decisions too.

I know how much you've helped me, you were patient and caring too.
I tried to make decisions on shirts and ties, and what I needed to do.
You cleared my thoughts, and helped me on my way,
I'm sure when your hours are up, you can truly say, "I have had a good day."

Dorothell Muldrow

I won't forget the lady who's behind the scene, who does the nice altering,
She does a great job on hemming, trimming, and doing all kinds of stitching.
Thank her for us, and let her know she does a great work,
And that she does it so nicely, and her work she does not shirk.

I'm ending this poem to say, I certainly enjoy writing for you,
God bless you much, Carla, and continue what you do.

APPRECIATION POEM FOR ANNIE

"The Language of friendship is not words but meanings."

- Henry David Thoreau

Annie, a long-time friendship we cherish so deeply,
We have kept up with each other, and it proves to be concretely.
I've enjoyed your cards, so unique and cute,
They had many regards for the right words to compute.

To include you in my gifted work,
Our friendship we will never shirk.
I will never forget way back in ST class,
How we studied together for the test we needed to pass.

You were called back to your job career, that you were waiting on,
But you never forgot me, and you kept in touch by card and by phone.
Those instructors were serious then, and had high expectations of us,
I lost my studying partner, but I made it through without so much as a fuss.

Thank you, Annie, for all you do,
God kept our friendship blessed and true.

Dorothell Muldrow

APPRECIATION POEM FOR CHERYL
at our Fiftieth Class Reunion

Thank you, Cheryl, for being a wonderful roommate,
We got to know each other very well; now you are more than a classmate.
Our conversations were interesting, in teaching each other's plight,
It gave support and direction, coming from the right source of light.

It's amazing how God's seasons come in your life,
Through others, He chooses to keep you from strife.
That's what you did for me Cheryl, from the moment we met,
Until the time we departed, you had me all set.

You put me in mind of your Mom, getting around and all,
You are leaving your mark in society, as you listen to your call.
You have a special gift, and my God put our visit in place,
A spirit knows a spirit, no negative, not a trace.

We will stay in touch, because I found a friend,
Not to rock your schedule, but just to talk and take in.
I will seek to find out where you are,
After knowing where you reside, you aren't very far.

Don't worry, I will not be in your door,
I will have my daughter find you for sure.
She won't worry you either, she will meet you to see,
What a great classmate you are, and she probably will agree.

On a Personal Note – Specialized Poetry for All Occasions

May God bless you Cheryl, in whatever route you take,
Doing what you do best with decisions you make.
Thanking God for you, for the time well spent,
There was consolation, and some things we could vent.
I truly enjoyed doing this poem for you,
Keep on being Cheryl, be blessed, be true.

Dorothell Muldrow

APPRECIATION POEM FOR DORIS AND STENETTA JOHNSON
and the CGMBC Willing Workers Ministry

To thank you for the lovely "Goody Bag," you gave it so specially,
You know just how to bring joy to someone, other than doing it verbally.
Starting with the angel, that set everything off with an awe,
Then the kind bow and the card, and the special garden scene on the bag I saw.

When I looked at the things that were in the bag,
There were so many treats, I felt I needed a price tag.
The ginger thins, the ginger candies, and right down to the ginger chews,
You covered me with many lifesavers and seeing the Mary Kay Satin Hand packets was very good news.

All that you gave me, has been a blessing indeed,
Even the wet ones, were a sure need.
I didn't forget the foaming hand soap with the fragrance of beach breeze,
You know just how to fix things up, and you do it with such ease.

Thank you again Doris and Stenetta, for your special gift ministry,
It certainly touched my heart and will inspire others pleasantly.
I enjoy the gift God gave me expressing my thoughts in prose,
I also enjoy featuring the gifts you gave me, and God truly knows.

I think of you Doris, how God lifted you and put you on a rock to stay,
He gave back well-being to you, and I know you will always cherish that every day.

On a Personal Note – Specialized Poetry for All Occasions

You are doing those special things now, that He had in store for you,
Thank you, Doris and Stenetta, for what I've received, what a nice blessing so true.

Let my words be a joy to those around me. Grace my speech with the light of your love. Amen.

Blessed

Dorothell Muldrow

APPRECIATION POEM TO DR. PARAMORE AND STAFF

Dr. Paramore, thank you so much for being so kind,
You diagnosed and did a great job on my cervical spine.
You fixated it with a foundation to stay,
When you told me what you would do, I was so dismayed that day.

But I went home and prayed, and came back and consented,
Being sure of my answer to go ahead, "Why prevent it?"
Wonderful surgery did take place,
I have no regrets upon my face.

Your office assistant "Levy," assured me it would work out just fine,
That you were meticulous in your efforts, and that you would clear all doubts from my mind.
I can say now, that my gait is with confidence,
Which I don't have to prove or convince.

I've gained back my stride with a cautious pep,
So glad about it each time I take a step.
A "BIG" thank you to your office staff for working the pre-admit testing, and surgical schedule for me,
Making sure of where to go and where I needed to be.

All the staff at the receptionist desk,
Presented themselves warmly and were at their best.
Thank you again Dr. Paramore, for being straight up with me,
Your integrity, handshake, and smile gave the guarantee.

Thank you, Dr. Paramore, job well done.

APPRECIATION POEM FOR JACQUELINE

The Lady of Benevolence

Jackie, just wanting to thank you, for all you've done for others,
You've shared so many things and it really helped those mothers.
Some didn't have much, and just used what they had,
For them to receive the items, gave them joy and made them so glad.

I myself retrieved a few pieces, that enhanced my attire,
It certainly worked really well for me, and prevented my buying desire.
I am so glad you are back at your home,
Because being elsewhere is not the norm.

Sometimes we lose what is dear to us,
But God redeems and restores it back, then it's good and just.
It helps us to appreciate the sunshine as well as the rain,
And when you and your family were patient, look what you've gained.

Be blessed Jackie and enjoy your new restored home,
You can rest easy now, no more to roam.

Thank you again, because it has been a blessing to many,
It is so good that it helped, and didn't cost not one penny.
Again, be blessed Jackie, and continue taking care of your mom and dad,
God is looking on, and the blessings He gives will always be more than you had.

Dorothell Muldrow

APPRECIATION POEM FOR LANELLE

"Friendship is the only cement that will ever hold the world together."

- Woodrow Wilson

Lanelle, a poem for you,
Because of your genuine friendship so true.
I wanted to include you in my gifted work,
Because our friendship, we never shirk.

I've noticed how well you'd worked and cared for your family,
Being young and very matured, you knew how to handle it contently.
There were many things on the job that weren't right,
But we sought what was good, while trusting God, we stayed in the fight.
I will never forget the baskets you made for me,
It started a friendship that honestly was meant to be.

Thank you for keeping in touch, you never failed to do that,
Even after you moved away adjusting to your new surroundings, you kept in contact.
So glad to include you in my special gift,
I hope it will give you an extra lift.
Our friendship is genuine indeed,

Won't ever forget the times in need.

On a Personal Note – Specialized Poetry for All Occasions

God put you in my spirit to share,
Because you are truly genuine and really care.

Dorothell Muldrow

APPRECIATION POEM FOR NANCY GORDON
My Physical Therapist

Gracious spirit, use my hands to help and heal. Use my actions, bold and meek, to be a vessel for you. May you be please to reveal your life to others through mine.
Thomas Lunch

Thank you Nancy, for such great therapy,
You rehabilitated my cervical spine so diligently.
I didn't know there were so many exercises,
Until I saw the layout, and there were no surprises.

God bless you for helping so many along,
The years you've given, God kept you strong.
More years to go, and strength God will give,
Keep up the good work, long as you live.

I will miss the therapy, which has been good for me,
It has helped me more, than I envisioned to see.
Your surgery was similar to mine, so you knew what was needed,
The small details we had to encounter, made us strong as God interceded.

I am glad about the surgery,
I've been truly blessed by the therapy.
Nancy, you are the greatest,
You have been kind and so worthy.

On a Personal Note – Specialized Poetry for All Occasions

To you Nancy Gordon, this poem of excellent work,
Not a given moment, did your work did shirk
Be ever blessed Nancy, take care of yourself,
Maybe I'll get to see you again, and it won't be as therapy needed for myself.

Dorothell Muldrow

APPRECIATION POEM TO REBECCA

Rebecca, Rebecca, sometimes I call you, "Becky,"
A friend that is so very dear.
You went through the fiery trials with me, and told me not to fear.

I thank you for being a friend, and how God use you to see me through,
It hadn't been easy, but I kept holding on, knowing what God could do.
You gave me encouragement, when I was feeling blue,
You said, "Dot, its going be alright. God will see you through."

Doesn't it feel good Becky, to be used by such a great God,
He needs those who will follow His lead, and tread the path Jesus trod.
You are a true friend Becky, with trials of your own,
We will fight the inevitable, because God is with us, and we are not alone.

Thank you for the quiet dwelling, which I needed truly so bad,
No distractions, no disturbances, it truly made me glad.
I spent some time with the Savior, and oh what a time I had,
He cleared some things in my mind, and there was nothing I could add.

So many things I did not understand, when God was refining me,
I tarried for a little while, then I saw what He wanted me to see.
I'm so glad I held on, so many times I felt the fall,
You really can't hurry God, He knows exactly what the "Call."

He built me up, and put me on a rock to stay,
I won't turn back, no matter what comes my way.
The fiery trials that tempt me now, can't compare to what I've

seen,
I am now content in the arms of the Savior, come what may,
whatever state I'm in.

I've had some tough moments, I almost thought I would die,
But holding on to the blood-stained banner gave me hope, and I kept willing to try.
Trying to stay focus, with an obstacle in place,
I thought about, "stick-to-it-faith," and remembered to seek God's face.

God graced me with His goodness, and with His kindness too,
Looking forward to my reward, with great strength and courage anew.

APPRECIATION POEM FOR TYWAN GOODSON

It gives me great pleasure, to do this poem for you,
Observing your kindness has been selfless, tried, and true.
You have proved yourself, through the things you say and do,
It shows in your effort, and your love for people too.

Being led to be a trustee, is the right calling for you,
You fit that position, to be trustworthy and helpful too.
Keep being an example, it will be a blessing, you'll see,
That is what God is looking for, and what you should be.

I don't know what more, God is planning for you,
Let your walk match your talk, and your blessings will come through.
Keep giving your heart to Jesus; continue what you do,
You won't go wrong with that, when you know God is watching you.

I look back on the times, when you brought your clients to Church,
You saw to their every need, in ways no one could touch.
I know you've been appreciated, in some milestone of your life,
You cared about your clients and kept them from misery and strife.

Stay focused, stay true to your calling; be conscious of doing the right thing,
God is always watching, and you never know what it will bring.

God's blessings in everything!

POEM FOR DR. RAY WILLIS – "THE HEALING HANDS"

I decided to write a poem for you, because it is what I do,
When I observe the most about someone, I put it in full view.
First of all, your granddad is proud, and is smiling down on you,
For following in his footsteps and doing those things he would do.

He would greet his clients with a smile, and would shake their hand,
Then inquire about how they are doing, of course, he would tell them how they stand.

You search their innermost thoughts, to figure out how to treat,
Then you place them on your special table, and those "healing hands" make it complete.
Well, what can I say? It is what it is, you are good at what you do,
You try the different methods, and before long, a change will come through.

Sabrina is your receptionist, and does a fine job each day,
Not only does she keep record, she moves the clients in and out without much delay.

I see honesty in your efforts, and you work toward meeting the need.
Helping those who are hurting, and rendering it with a good deed.

You have a wonderful family, with four beautiful kids;
What God has joined together will grow, without any bids.

Dr. Ray, you have that boyish look, and is handsome as can be,
Don't forget, "handsome is, as handsome does;" being faithful is wise, and that's the key.

Dorothell Muldrow

MRS. DENNIS, LADY OF ENDURING FAITH

It is good that one should hope Great is your faithfulness. **(Lam. 3:22-23)**

Oh! What a lady of enduring faith, to overcome the whelms of life,
Your optimism shows you have a high regard for the Savior, that buffers the misery and strife.
You were a jetsetter once, and did many things that you enjoyed,
You reminisce about them now, with fond memories that you can't avoid.

You did a lot of good, even when things were bad,
You met them all with Christ in mind, the best friend you ever had.
You are a mailer of cards, touching those who are in mind,
Most of all you enjoy being around people;
And people are for each other to be helpful and kind.
Heidi is your close-knit friend, she stays close underfoot,
She watches every step you make;
Never to leave you, and that's by the animal's book.

Just a few words Mrs. Dennis, to describe the lady I see,
You are a special and loving lady, which is the best way to be.
To include you in my personalized, published poem book,
From time to time, you can take a look.

MY TEACHER FRIEND, BETSY BIRD

You are going away, my teacher friend, to a place close to family;
We will miss you oh so dearly; but it's not endingly.
God gave you a season for teaching; He said, "Betsy, it's time to rest, I've found someone whom I can trust; don't worry, I've picked the best!" (Kathy)

God saw you through a journey; and Jim has to go through his still,
Don't worry Betsy, God knows what He's doing; just trust Him to do His will.
Maybe sometimes you will email me, or even send a note in the mail,
While sitting quietly in thought, remembering your work unveil.

We thank God for His Goodness, in all that He has done,
We thank Him for His kindness, and the victory through you He's won.

Thank you, Betsy, for touching my heart through God's word.
I won't forget you.

Dorothell Muldrow

THE PEE DEE BAPTIST ASSOCIATION OF CHRISTIAN EDUCATION

In appreciation from the class to Pastor Cecil Bromell for sharing so many things on how to rightly divide the word of truth and how it is to be used to ready His people. - Fall Bible Institute

Location: Ebenezer M. B. Church SHEREC Building.

To Our Teacher and President Pastor Cecil Bromell
Subject: The Preacher and the Call of God

From the class:
Pastor Bromell, once more you have taught us well,
You've shared with us so much that we can surely tell.
This was another class of building good soil,
You cultivated and planted good seed, now we are fit for our Call.
You said to us, "God called us to grow the ministry, to speak hope and not misery and strife,"
And that we are God's mouthpiece, to help those with uncertainty of life.
Just like the Prophets you named: Isaiah, Jeremiah, Ezekiel, and the Herdsman Amos,
We were to see if the Prophet's calling identifies with any of us.
On Isaiah's Call, he had seen God's Glory, and acknowledged his unclean lips,
The people that he'd dwelled with, let us know we fall short and have many slips.
God's Call on Jeremiah, was designated before he was formed,
Jeremiah says, "Ah Lord God, I am too young, I'm not skilled to speak, I can't perform.
But God said, "Go and say what I tell you to say,"

God touched his mouth, gave him courage, and he was on his way.
Ezekiel heard a voice from God, told him where he was to go,

On a Personal Note – Specialized Poetry for All Occasions

God said, "The people were unreasonable and stubborn, but the instructions I will give you will show."

God said, "To speak my word to the people whether they listen or refuse,"
To not be rebellious like them, but to open your mouth with no excuse.
God's Call on Amos, a Herdsman and fig grower. He was wondering why me?
God said to him, "Go and prophesy to my people Israel, no respecter I have, can't you see?"

Amos 5:24 says, "*Let Judgment run down as waters and righteous as a mighty stream*,"
God indeed intend for His instructions to go forward, no matter to what extreme.
Pastor Bromell, you gave us much surgical background, and the need of a skill practitioner,
Sometimes we need cutting, sometimes we need therapy, and sometimes we just need our God, our soul discerner.

You said to be useful, that we may be that arm in the community we'll make,
And it will be a great fulfillment and blessing, that will go far beyond a paycheck.
Thank you, Pastor Bromell, for one more lesson to shape us and to grow,
We must not leave it here in the classroom, but like God sent His Prophets, we must go!

Dorothell Muldrow

Section Two

Children

EQUIP(MEANT) TO BE: A POEM FOR ANTHONY

This is a message for you that I did in the form of a poem.
I hope you will like it, and it'll make you feel right at home.

God is preparing you for some things right now,
To equip and strengthen your way;
I don't know where He will carry you,
But be ready, stay focused, and pray.

He's providing you with what you need,
To carry out what matters in your life;
It is a preventative measure to keep you from misery and strife.

It will build character that you'll need at home,
It will make improvements and blessings will surely come.
The truck has been giving you trouble, and what a hold up it's been;
God knows all about it, and is ready to defend.

Everything you're experiencing will soon become alright;
It will make you think more wisely, even when things are in a tight.

God is able and is willing, and is always by your side;
Imagine Him being in the seat next to you,
Being your grace, your compass, and your guide.

We love you "Ant" with all our heart,

Dorothell Muldrow

And we love your family tree;
So what I've said along and along,
Is equip(meant)to be...

Take all of this in account my son,
Digest it if you can;
God has not forsaken you,
So be wise, take heed, be a man.

Love you. Mom.

A POEM FOR MY DAUGHTER INGELL

Hi, my daughter Ingell, a daughter of my dream,
I thank God for you my daughter; of great strength and esteem.
I observe your life so vividly, of how you move through your highs and lows,
Being a lady of strength and vigor, and a description that most people knows.

You've done a great job with your life, you've conquered it one on one,
You always say, "Be encouraged, victory will be won."
You have grown in stature and might,
You were encouraged to stay in the fight.
God will unfold it, and it will be alright.
He's got His eyes on you, and you're never out of sight.

I've written this poem for you, to say a few things I've observed,
I remember when we almost lost you to sickness, but, God said, "No, there's more she deserves."
Oh, I'm so glad about it, because it was for a reason,
You will change many hearts, and you are in your season.

You are patiently waiting, for God to unfold,
The move for your life, that is still untold.
God will do it, and unfold it in His time,
Trust and obey, it won't cost you a dime.

I love you my daughter Ingell, for all the things you do,
Thank you for being my daughter and thank you for being you.

I love you very much, and God loves you even more.

Dorothell Muldrow
A POEM FOR MY OLDEST SON MARK
My Loving Son for your Encouragement

Mark, I am doing this poem for you, because this is what I do,
I observe some things and sometimes, God just gives me a view.
Mark, you are seeking and cannot find it, because of your insight,
Once in a while, take a moment to be still, and you will get it all right.

God has taken good care of you,
Now He's waiting for you to come through.
When looking back over your life to see,
What went wrong to alter your blessings to be.

I know what it is, your innermost need,
To reconcile with self, then God will intercede.
Quiet your spirit, get in line,
Take the scales off your eyes and be inclined.

Mark, have no regrets, and no holds bar,
Your wounds will be healed, so there won't be any scars.
Gird up your loins, with courage anew,
Look forward to this new discovery, that is waiting for you.

You are holding it up, because of this other view,
You know what God wants; He doesn't want those other things;
He wants you,
Discover the deep things of God, let them shine through,
Reach way, way down, He'll pick you up,
With more blessings that were due.

If you believe that this can happen…It will depend upon you,
You must fight the inevitable, you can do it "Mark-a-boo."
My God has taken good care of you,
He shadowed your footsteps and kept your mind too.

On a Personal Note – Specialized Poetry for All Occasions

You have so much to be thankful for, when you think of the things you've been through,
The changes, the mishaps, the let downs, and thought patterns too.
Don't be afraid to step out, your discovery is in place,
It's up to you my son, take the leap, it will be your pace.

I know you have thought many things, over and over,
Things you want to change inside, that you no longer want to cover.
There have been struggles, that brought you much pain,
So glad that you realized through those struggles, what you now will gain.

God picked you up, and turned you around,
He gave you a better thought pattern, to keep you level on ground.
God will walk you through it, and He's always by your side,
All you have to do is believe it will happen, stay calm, and abide.

It has been a pleasure to do this poem for you,
I love you so much, and want things to work for you too.
These words will give you good footing, and encouragement also,
Remember, God says, not to worry;
You got Jesus, and that's for sure.

Dorothell Muldrow

Section Three

Grandchildren Poems

A POEM FOR MY GRANDDAUGHTER ANTHONAE

Personal and Special

I wrote this poem for you Anthonae, to say we enjoyed your visit with us.
I watched you as you be yourself, you slept most of the day, and I did not fuss.

I wrote this in a poem, in hopes it would interest you,
To do some writing for yourself, when you're at a low and feeling blue.
You would be amazed when you put your mind to it, of things you didn't think you could do,
It happened for me one day, in amazement of this blessing so true.

You are tall for your age Anthonae, so much like I was,
With less to do, you just take a chair, and softly pause.
Like most young people, you like the phone, to keep you occupied and content,
But it was taken from you, for a time;
You didn't like it, but the time off it, was well spent.

Your phone was taken from you, because of something you did,
You played the hide-and-seek game, and discovered where it was hid.

That's alright Anthonae, this will hurt you, but will also help,
It will grow you up to realize, you can do without, so you just as well accept.

I learned so much about you, the two weeks you spent here,
I like nurturing you in the right direction, it should have been that

Dorothell Muldrow

we live near.
I hoped that I'd helped you, somewhat… maybe a lot,
Life can be confusing, remember you can always count on,
Grandma Dot.

How many times you hear, "I love you, Anthonae?"
"I love you," from Grandma, and more is on the way.
I love you enough, for you are my granddaughter, and that outweighs for me,
I'd love to see you better your life, and be all that you can be.

I looked at your bucket and shovel, it reminds me of the enjoyment you once had,
Watching you at the park that day, brought back memories so glad.
"Baby girl" which I call your sister, loves to be around and near you,
Be an example, that she would want to be like…
Then one day, you can look back and say, "I had no clue."

I like to see y'all as a family, get up and go to church,
Sunday school is preference, I'd like to see that much.
It would be good to get the knowledge of our Lord, and that's cool!
You can get more about life at church, than in school.

So it's up to you Anthonae, to stop sharing some things with friends,
They will only look at you different, and not understand the trends.
I hope you have resolved, the things that you admitted to,
All you need is a made-up mind, and you will surely make it through.

It's not easy to succumb, or erase what has happened to you,
But I know a Savior, who will erase it, and be there for you too.
You first must believe it, no matter what one says,
Even if you depart from friends, you don't need those ways.

On a Personal Note – Specialized Poetry for All Occasions

Quiet time is essential, just to think things through.
But not too much of that, it will make you wonder too.
I want you to dig deep in your lessons, make good grades if you can,
Keep reading your Bible every day, for you Anthonae, God has a plan.
You are to be a mighty warrior, to combat the inevitable with a smile.
Satan will not have your life, be true to yourself, and go that extra mile.

Do you hear me Anthonae? This is your Grandma Dot speaking,
You are going to be fine, long as you know what you are seeking.
I remind you again, good things you will find,
It's up to you to not go back, but forward you go, and keep all good things in mind.

I love you Anthonae, Grandma Dot.

Dorothell Muldrow

A POEM FOR MY GRANDDAUGHTER MCKENZIE

"Kenzie," you are my youngest grandchild, and especially unique,
You are very intelligent and has much wit to keep us on our feet.
You were my helpmate in the kitchen, you wash dishes after the meal,
You did it without grumbling, you were so seriously…for real.

You always kept us smiling, with the things you would say,
You were so particular about your dress each day.
You met up with this cat, that was friendly at first,
Until he scratches your hand, the only thing he got was something for thirst.

He was not a pretty cat, and was hungry all the time,
You would feed him the bones I gave you, then all he would do was climb.

I miss you "Baby Girl" from being around,
Looking forward to your next visit, to make us smile, and to be our special clown.

Thank you for being my helper, it meant a lot to me,
Sometimes, I had to correct you, it was in love I'm sure you could see.
Do your homework, all that you can,
Find the time to help mommy,
Cause she's your #1 fan.

Don't cause your mommy to fuss, because it is not good for her,
Do as she ask, be honest and true, because she really cares.
Go to bed on time, don't forget your prayer,
Never, never forget about it, you must always keep it near.

On a Personal Note – Specialized Poetry for All Occasions

God will hear your prayer, each time you want to say it,
God never gets tired, don't you worry, God loves it, every little bit.
Pray for mommy and daddy, also your sisters too,
Your brothers need prayer also, add them to the list, please do.

So "Baby Girl" I will close for now, sending a kiss on the forehead,
Be good in every way and remember the things I said.

A POEM FOR MY GRANDDAUGHTER JORDAN

Jordan, my lovely granddaughter, has grown to be on your own,
I'm proud that you are striving, to go at it alone.
I know you are looking after your mother, and you've done that very well,
And I know you are making a life for yourself, and I know it will be something to tell.

You know that I love you Jordan, and this poem will speak it plain,
It's about your beautiful life, that you will not live in vain.
I am using my gift of poetry, and this is what God enables me to do,
It may interest you to do this yourself one day, finding a gift so true.

Be mindful of your friendships, to keep them in the right view,
Look at the assignment that I'm giving you, it will correct and renew.
It speaks about heeding the principles that God adorned,
Remember you are special in His sight, ever since you were born.

It's all in the Bible, read **Romans 1:18-32**,
It reveals God's word of judgment upon this world so true.
They say life is short; I believe it's nearer as it seems,
Because of the way the world has gone wrong, and things are done to the extreme.

On a Personal Note – Specialized Poetry for All Occasions

A sweet word to you Jordan, because that's what God has me to do,
I hope I'm planting a loving seed, please share it with your friends too.
I love you very dearly, and will always tell you so,
God will credit me for telling you these things, in hopes it will help to grow.

To grow in the wisdom of what is right,
Yearning to walk and talk, living in the light.
Lean not to your feelings of your own understanding,
It will be rewarding, selfless, and truly amending.

Your life can be the greatest, because you are a gift from God,
Please do treat your body as it is in His image, and you will walk the path Jesus trod.
Don't even think about those things that you messed up on,
You know Jesus has taken care all of that, and the battle has been won.
God is good like that; unconditional love,
He is the only one who can do that, straight from Heaven above.

Always look forward, keep focus on Eternity,
These things that are taken place, are only temporary.
He's patient and He's kind, and gives you immeasurable chances,
He will pick you right up, and still give you advances.

You are my precious, granddaughter of choice,
You look so much like me on my girl picture I came across.
So gird up your loin, and you will get it right,
God loves you, and will woo you, to the direction of His light.

I truly enjoyed writing this poem for you,

Dorothell Muldrow

Continue in your plight, and your blessings will come through.
I love you, I love you, I love you very much,
I hope you will be attentive, and please keep in touch.

Section Four

Anniversary Poems

Dorothell Muldrow

A POEM FOR OUR PASTOR'S ANNIVERSARY 2018

Pastor's Anniversary of E. B. Burroughs

55 years of *pastoralship*, which is very unique in itself,
The church family presents to you this service, that doesn't have to go on a shelf.
Just relax and enjoy, what we have for you this day,
Just be ready to except all what will come your way.
55 years of *pastoralship*, which God has embraced so well,
God's grace has been sufficient through the years, we all can tell.

Endurance plays a big part, being available when it took much effort,
Of course, your teaching and preaching are always sufficient, and always gets a great report.
Very few Sundays you've missed, and that's a lot to be thankful for,
God kept you strong when the times were hard, and when you didn't feel up to par.
We are so glad to celebrate with you these 55 Pastorate years,
These were years that was never wasted, even through the sweat and tears.
These also been years of challenge, and we know who you counted on,
God kept your lamps trimmed and burning, and He's the one that says, "Well done."

You have a loving first lady, that has been by your side all the way,
God has also kept her strong, and she's by your side today.
We wish you well Pastor Burroughs, and we appreciate this 55-year tenure,
Enjoy all we do for you, and look forward to your new season renewal.

AN ANNIVERSARY POEM FOR CHARLES AND LAMAR

This is a loving moment to wish you well,
For another anniversary that God has wrought you to tell.
The years have been sown, the battles have been won,
You will keep on winning and realize what God has done.

Just to still be here celebrating another year,
We all are so blessed with God's love, oh, so sincere.
We look ahead, taking one day at a time,
No worry, no hurry, just appreciating our prime.

God has been gracious to you through sickness and health,
You've thanked God for small things, and that's better than wealth.
Through many years of ebb and flow,
God whispered sweet peace and said, "I am with you as you go."
Charles and Lamar, you have thanked God for the years,
It's brought about strength of your love that cares.
God bless your Anniversary today,
May God sustain you in every way.

Many blessings to you both.

Dorothell Muldrow

Section Five

Poems

A POEM TO MY BIRTHDAY (SAKE)
BARB THAYER

Happy birthday Barb, and thank you for the E-Card,
You have been a blessing when things for me were hard.
You helped me to develop the skills that I am carrying today,
It has enhanced my efforts, and increased writings have come my way.

I am composing many poems. I've been encouraged to do a book,
I don't know where this all may lead, but I know it has me on a hook.
I find myself writing much in a poetic way,
I truly enjoy each poem I write, which will bring a smile or ray.

God has given me this gift of writing, and I know He's writing them too,
As He continues to order my steps, He will show me what to do.
I thank God for the gift, and for sending help my way,
I could never ever claim no other, but God's grace today.

I hoped your day was pleasant. I tried to reach you today,
It's never too late to get this birthday message on the way.
I know Joel celebrated with you. He is such a good husband to you,
You deserve this birthday milestone, and all the ado.

Blessings and more blessings to you Barb.

Dorothell Muldrow

A BIRTHDAY POEM FOR KIM

Happy Birthday to you, Kim! And many more to come,
Oh what joy and glee, with the smile on your face, and then some.
How special this milestone; the years of stature and might,
Where do you think it came from? None other than the Good Lord, that's right-t-!!

Kim, you have wit about you, and a gift of sensible gab too,
It's in great expectation, keeping us smiling, while wit fully keeping it true.
Your family and friends are here, celebrating this special milestone,
God has granted you this special day, on the very day you were born.

Continue your walk, let it match your talk, Kim.
Listen to the voice of God, and keep your wits about Him.
Continue being happy, loving others as you do,
Remember to stay focused, God will be pleased with you.

A POEM FOR MARQUIS, CELEBRATING HIS 50TH BIRTHDAY

Happy Birthday, to you "Mark!" You've reached a special milestone,
This was already destiny, right from the day you were born.
Marquis Delaine, is your given name, "Mark" is what we call you most of the time,
You've grown up to be a man my son, now that you are 50, you are now in your prime.

"Mark" is what we call you for short, "Penugy," is what we would call you as a boy,
Whatever we called you, we would see you smile, and it would bring much joy.

"Mark," you made the 50-year mark, with God right by your side,
Only the Good Lord being within, will keep you and to teach you to abide.
We know it was not easy, with the struggles that you had,
Dealing with the customers and cars, and the weather when bad.

We know God made all things good, this is not a complaint,
We know about struggles, and how God use them to put us in constraint.
God knows what you need, better than you will ever know yourself,
Sometimes we understand better after we say, "Hey, it's myself!"

You will say, "I am made in God's image, and He loves me just as I am,
God makes no mistake, He will use me as His ram."
Enjoy your birthday "Mark," take it in stride,
Remember, God is your foothold, and let Him only, be your guide.

Dorothell Muldrow

A BIRTHDAY POEM FOR TERESA

Happy Birthday, Teresa! And all that it will bring,
God's blessings are among them; He is our everything.
Good friends and lovely family are here, to help you celebrate,
This wonderful occasion of joy, that no one can even rate.

Happy Birthday, Teresa! And many more to come,
You've reached a milestone these 55 years, and you know where it came from.
There have been times of trials; God brought you through them all,
These 55 years, God's blessed you; and He won't let you fall.

I know this day means a lot, where we joined in unity,
It makes the atmosphere very pleasant, with much love, joy, and glee.
I brought to you this lovely poem, to cheer you and to say,
Happy! Happy Birthday, Teresa! And enjoy your special day.

AN 80TH BIRTHDAY POEM FOR DEACON JEROME GOODSON

A poem of celebration of an 80-year plight,
A portrait of a person of great vigor and might.
A man of stature, "Deacon Jerome," you wear it well,
By your kindness and your favor that most people can tell.

You give so much in commitment, which is always in place,
We can always count on you, we need no back up just in case.
A true Deacon, and a man of worth,
We need more character like yours upon this earth.

When you moved back home, and connected with the church,
God said, "There's a man I can use; it will be without a search."
You met your wife Brenda, someone to be by your side,
She brought much happiness into your life, with much love that abide.

The year you became deathly ill, and the doctor shook his head,
The sad news that we'd received, that you would soon be dead.
But God stepped in and said, "There are some specifics that I've found,
This situation will be altered and completely turned around."

God said, "I am here for you,"
And you will live instead of the doctor's view.
"Deacon Jerome," You came already made,
The plans God had for you were already laid.

The brush of death, the extended years,
The unique way with words, no regretting tears.
I'm glad you are still here "Deacon Jerome," by the grace of God,
You can still lead the path that Jesus trod.

Dorothell Muldrow

This is an occasion of a beautiful plight,
Of you "Deacon Jerome," and everything is such a delight.
Just relax, be spoiled, and take it in stride,
Things are so elegant, so please enjoy the ride.

Your family and friends are here, also many church members too,
To join in this milestone, of long life anew.
God bless you "Deacon Jerome," for still being here,
With strength not of your own, but only God's to bear.

Your years have been blessed, no doubt about it,
Your activity, your mind, thanking God for every bit.
That's who you are, "Deacon Jerome,"
More added blessings, before reaching your heavenly home.

Continue being true to yourself, letting God lead the way,
And your record with God, will be displayed one day.

ANNETTE'S BIRTHDAY POEM

Happy Birthday, Annette! You've reached another milestone,
God has granted you another year. See, what God has done?
This is a celebration of a day that God has made,
Where we join with family and friends, with enjoyment being shed.

Annette, your abilities may be altered, and you may be moving slow,
But, remember God's grace is sufficient, and He's everywhere you go.

These are our best days, each time we awake,
Give God all the glory and honor, be happy for goodness sake.
You keep right on pushing forward; think positive in your mind,
God sees and knows what you go through, and will never leave you behind.

You are an inspiration, and when you speak, we listen well.
You bring thoughts from your heart, that only you can tell.
Enjoy this special day, and let God be your guide,
This is the day that the Lord has made! It's your birthday! Take it in stride.

In loving memories of Annette Muldrow.

CELEBRATING ONE MORE YEAR OF A BEAUTIFUL LIFE

One more year of a beautiful life, with much thanksgiving and praise;
Only God can cultivate this milestone, in leaps and bounds, and so many ways.
Carrie, this celebration is most pleasant, and much joy is in the air;
Wonderful friends and family are here, to enjoy and bring you cheer.

Your gifted talent is all around, with its brilliant colors so nice,
Each has its own personality, with a detail of none done twice.
Oh what glee, and fun to share, on this celebrated day;
Butterflies and flowers, expressing God's beauty on display.

Some may be the same color, but different in some way,
Handmade by you Carrie, look how great a display.
Using your gifted abilities, putting them into play,
Our God can do anything, and can use us in anyway.

God gives us wonderful inventions, expressing His will to achieve;
Carrie, you've been consistent in your efforts, never knowing what you would receive.

Keep on going forward doing things according to His will,
You don't know where it will lead, He has many blessings still.
Enjoy this celebration, let your joy be known;
God made you in His image, let His light and joy be shown.

God bless you Carrie, and all that are assembled here,
To celebrate one more beautiful and joyful year.

A BIRTHDAY AND APPRECIATION POEM FOR A SPECIAL TEACHER/ FRIEND

There is a word for you Carolyn, a word of gratitude,
Of all the things you taught me, without an attitude.
I said that because of your patience, when you could have shushed me to the side,
Saying, "No help! for this one, Lord I've tried."

You taught with such wit, and kept smiles on each face,
We would never get bored, because you taught with the right pace.
Oh, how I miss your classes, and seeing you at your best;
It was so much fun, looking forward to each test.

God has kept you strengthened on this journey for a while,
He knows your ability and covers your extra mile.
Sometimes I wish to be near, to do it all over again,
To sit in your presence and brush up to sustain.

I think about you often, whenever I do a speech,
To make sure my words are in order and maintain what you did teach.
You are celebrating this special day that God has granted you,
You will see friends and family and many blessings too.

This is a birthday poem for you and appreciation too,
I am grateful to have this ability, which is from God through you.
You stirred up this gift in me, and I know you smoothed it out.
I was so dumbfounded and made so many mistakes.
You corrected me along the way;
Now look what difference it makes.

Dorothell Muldrow

Enjoy your celebration, continued blessings to you,
You are very special;
Keep doing the things you do.

A POEM FOR BETTY'S 65TH BIRTHDAY CELEBRATION

Happy 65th birthday Betty, God has blessed you once more,
You've reached a milestone in this life; one more blessing than before.
You've made so many happy, making them smile along the way,
You make them laugh! You make them grin! And oh, what else can I say?

You have such a bubbly way that brings joy to our hearts,
Your smile, the funny things you say, keeps our spirit in tune, not apart.
Keep being yourself and let God be your guide,
You won't have to worry; because He is by your side.

You have such a great family, and your friends seem to be too,
They have brought you joy and cheer; and truly came through for you.
God bless and keep you Betty, in the times that are ahead,
He's got a hedge all around you; nothing more can be said.

We were glad to help celebrate this milestone of your day,
And it is not all over; more blessings are on the way.
I wrote this poem for you, to cheer you and to say,
65 years and grateful and enjoy your special day.

Dorothell Muldrow

A BIRTHDAY POEM FOR BERTHA "PC"

Happy Birthday! Bertha, and what a wonderful day,
Being with friends and family, to bring joy and cheer your way.
Another year, another birthday, and another day older,
Bertha, you're looking very well, with your colorful hues upon your shoulder.

I like the different colors, and glasses that you wear,
Including your accessories, oh how they bring us cheer.
You wear pastel colors and rose colors, also a little grey maybe some blue,
Sometimes flora patterns, with a little citrus in the hue.

Whatever the color or attire you wear, certainly brings about a happy conversation and much cheer.
Hey! This is not about the colors or the attire you wear,
It's about you and your birthday, these other things just happen to appear.

You truly brighten the corner where you normally are,
And you certainly aren't by yourself,
You have a friend that is close to your heart, that you cannot put upon a shelf.

It's a friend in Jesus, who is our closest friend supreme,
Allow your colors to be like Him, making sure it sends out the right beam.

You are always smiling, and making someone smile,
You keep moving right along, doing the extra mile.

You surely bring lots of fun, and please don't let anyone make you mad,

On a Personal Note – Specialized Poetry for All Occasions

Most folk know who you are, a different kind of fun that we never had.
Well, I certainly enjoyed writing a few things about you,
Of things that I observed to be absolutely true.

Keep that corner brighten with good things, and many blessings will come through.

A BIRTHDAY POEM FOR "PAT"

God has granted you this beautiful day, to celebrate another year,
Take it in stride, one moment at a time, be joyous and happy with cheer.

You have crossed the extra mile, with faith to stay in the race;
Enduring your ups and downs, when keeping up your pace.

You have grown so much in God's grace, with the songs that touch our hearts;
Singing, "I Found the Answer" I learned to pray, which will ward off those fiery darts.

You care so much for family, meeting their every need,
Sometimes in running an errand, or to help with some gathering to feed.
Whatever task it is, you are right there in place,
To render the services, whatever you face.

Sometimes God will rest you, and sometimes He'll test you too;
He is always there to make things better, and be right there to bring you through.
God has such a beautiful way, that He works out the plans in life,
With patience, strength, and courage, which keeps us grounded from strife.

God has been most gracious to you, through sickness, health, and then some.
I'm so glad you're having this birthday…be thankful, be cheerful!
There are more blessings and birthdays to come.

A BIRTHDAY POEM FOR BRAXTON

Start by doing what's necessary, then what's possible, and suddenly you are doing the impossible. - Francis of Assisi

I had you in mind to write some kind words about you,
You, my grandson, makes it easy to do.
You are forever so kind to touch base,
It's good to do that just in case.

I always say character is one thing people will remember when they are gone,
Be it attitude, selflessness, discipline, self-discovery, since you were born.
You want to leave an impressive character behind,
And for it to be one of the best ones, anyone can find.

I like the way you look after your sisters,
They look to their big brother too;
You're not able to see them all the time,
But you know just what to do.

You are sticking with the job, which is a good thing,
It gives you security, money in your pocket, and other things to bring.
Showing responsibility can become one day a legacy,
Having the endurance and beating the odds is good policy.

"The Culinary Art," has been put on hold, but you'll pick it back up,
Sometimes other things will come into the picture that can interrupt.
Just a few words of my encouraging poetry;
This is what I do,
Being a sower of seeds my grandson, hoping to grow many good things in you.

Dorothell Muldrow

A BIRTHDAY POEM FOR CARRIE

Carrie you've made another birthday,
With smiles and much esteem,
How did you like your surprise?
Did it bring happiness supreme?

The children are so gracious,
To do this blessed thing;
To the one that they love so much,
And what joy it will bring.

Do you feel any younger?
As you know it added a year;
Just don't worry so much about it,
This is what happens… Please, don't shed a tear.

You are young at heart and vibrant,
As you go from day to day;
Doing the things you like to do,
And whatever comes your way.

I brought you this fun message,
To cheer you and to say;
Happy Birthday Carrie!
And enjoy your special day.

A POEM FOR MY BROTHER-IN-LAW CLARENCE FOR HIS 80TH BIRTHDAY CELEBRATION

Clarence, you've made a milestone; these 80 wonderful years,
80 years of grace and mercy; knowing how God cares.
You never know what God will give; but you trusted Him along the way,
You did not reach these many years; on your own, I must say.

You did a little farming, with all of your might,
I look at the parked tractor, with a landmark of memories so bright.
You still do gardening, in the morning sun,
Gathering and sharing the goods; after the work is done,

You sit under the tree shade, to watch your garden grow,
Thanking God for the effort, and all the seeds to sow.
God's given you the ability, to do things each day,
Aren't you glad no more hard work, no more forking of the hay?

God gave you many years, and you've had some highs and lows,
You kept right on moving, and God kept opening doors.
Your family and friends are here, to celebrate this wonderful birthday,
God will grant you best wishes, and many returns today.

Clarence, enjoy this wonderful milestone; give God all the praise,
Be grateful for God's glory; that is shown in so many ways.
God bless you Clarence, my brother-in- law;
Be strong, be brave, be true;
I thank you for being my brother-in- law; and all the things you do. God forever bless you.

Dorothell Muldrow

A BIRTHDAY POEM FOR MAE ALICE

What a pleasure it is to write this poem about you,
For a person that I admire, with fun and optimism too.
I value your kindness, and all the things you do,
It only brings out the person, that is sincere and true.

There is much admiration, from your family and dear friends,
Because you go the extra mile, with the blessings God sends.
You have been through a journey, and still are tested at times;
Give God praises and honor! Applaud Him! That's no crime.

God has blessed you abundantly, from being content to the blessings of more,
You always know what to do with them, for God's blessings are for sure.

This is your birthday celebration, with special people all around,
No one can beat friends and kinfolks, with their laughter and such joyous sound.
This is such a wonderful occasion, and so much fun is in the air,
Folks are moving around being helpful, with so much love and care.
Hearing the cheerful sounds of the people, as they fellowship,
Their laughter and smiles, only God can equip.

You move so humbly in your actions, taking care of matters as they come,
Knowing it's not easy all the time, and wonder where they all came from.
Don't worry and don't you fret; God's got it all in control,

On a Personal Note – Specialized Poetry for All Occasions

God handle many problems, and all that will unfold.

God will not take lightly, of the things you try to do,
Because your heart is willing, and God will surely favor you.
God bless you Mae Alice, you have pressed the extra mile,
God has given you another wonderful year, to celebrate with a smile.

So happy! Happy birthday! And more blessings from above,
God doesn't have to do this, but that's the God we love.

Dorothell Muldrow

A BIRTHDAY POEM FOR MRS. HERLINA D. MORRIS

When He comes, in that day, to be glorified in His saints and to be admired among all those who believe, because our testimony among you was believed.
(2 Thessalonians 1:10)

Happy birthday "Mrs. Herlina," the lady of a "robust" life,
You keep right on moving without much strife.
Mrs. Herlina, you've done well, and have fitted right in,
God sent along a strong arm, "Terry," to be with you now and then.

You've made your home on a wonderful crepe myrtle street,
Right down from your new home church, which is very close to meet.
You work well with the, "Senior Saints" and it means so much to each,
This ministry is not only bonding, it is also there to teach.

Friends and loved ones are celebrating you today,
On your 87th birthday with many blessings on the way.
Some call you "Herlina," some call you "Doll,"
Today you are called "Birthday Girl" No fuss, not even a quarrel.

God has granted you 87 wonderful years,
All were not all up hill, and you've had some tears.
God has always been with you, and there's no doubt about it,
You are still here by the grace of God, with reasonable health and reasonable physical fit.

Keep looking up Mrs. Herlina, God is always there,
You can truly count on Him, because He is always near.
Mrs. Herlina, continue being ever so sweet,
Enjoy this beautiful day of celebration, it is such a treat.
Many more birthdays I hope you see,
God will certainly grant it to be.

Dorothell Muldrow

A BIRTHDAY POEM FOR SADIE – A LONGTIME FRIEND

Happy Birthday, Sadie! And what a lovely day,
God has granted you a blessing, and more is on the way.
You are a courageous lady, and it has not been easy all the time,
But God in His business, will bring you peace sublime (inspiring awe).

Sadie, you shuffle your hours between getting the children to school and back,
And those other things you do in between, hasn't given you much slack.
You meet the needs of others, God sees all that you do,
He holds you up and keeps you and gives you strength to go through.

You look after your family tree, with God's grace and might,
The journey has not been easy, but God always makes it alright.
Kyle is growing to be a young man now, and oh how you have withstood,
God has granted you that special attachment to him, and you've done well as you should.
Shayla is a fine young lady, God's got something special coming her way,
Patience is the key word for right now, we must wait and believe all that He say.

Sadie, you have a special gift, that you only can understand,
Most people get to see it, but only God knows what brand.

On a Personal Note – Specialized Poetry for All Occasions

Keep on trusting and believing God for His will and plan,
I see the flourishing flower blooming in you, that only God can.

Enjoy your birthday "2017," and all you will receive,
Keep right on loving God and always keep the faith and believe.
Love you Sadie, with all of my heart,
Friendships are special, and we had that right from the start.

Dorothell Muldrow

AN APPRECIATION AND 80TH BIRTHDAY POEM FOR OUR PASTOR

Pastor Burroughs, this is your day of a wonderful milestone.
We look at your accomplishments and say, how time has passed and gone.
You've done lots of great things, across the many miles,
Gaining success and accolades, some tears and some smiles.

You have many of friends and family here, to celebrate this special day,
Just take it in stride, relax and smile, you deserve all that is coming your way.
The folks are moving around with much admiration and glee,
They all feel good about what they are doing;
You can look around and see.

You are a great teacher and preacher, allowing the Holy Spirit to lead,
God granted you a very long life, and will give you more of what you need.
You've been great with your calling, giving wisdom when called upon,
God has given you strength and courage, without God's grace, this could not be done.

You pursued more education to bring to us what is best,
You never ceased to give up, though sometimes trials will come as a test.
You keep right on moving, persevering to whatever may come,

Knowing God's got your back, with a purpose, a plan, and then some.

Happy 80th Birthday! Pastor Burroughs,
And enjoy your special day;
Be grateful for God's Divine love and blessings He has brought your way.

Dorothell Muldrow

Section Six

Welcome Farewell! Poems

A WELCOME POEM FOR THE CLASS OF '66

50TH Class Reunion

Hello classmates, it's good to see you all,
We are going to have fun, in fact, we're going to have a ball.
Looking at faces that I haven't seen in a while,
So good to see all of you; your faces, also your smiles.

These 50 years, God has blessed us really good,
And we are still here, in spite of the many things withstood.
It's good to see the gathering, looking good as we must,
And those many things we withstood, all have been kicked to the dust.

We are blessed to have a reasonable portion of health and strength,
We've all have had some kind of struggles, but we trusted God, and He gave us more length.

I say you are looking good my classmates, we are moving right along
We are alive and have our being, can't even, or won't complain that anything is wrong.
We are so gracious to be together, although we lost some our classmates to death,
But we are grateful for life in itself, and that is somewhat better than wealth,

We hope to see more years to come, as God wills it for us,
Just be glad for each day, with plenty of peace, contentment, and no fuss.
I love you classmates with all my heart,
And sorry this wonderful occasion, we'll soon depart,
God has blessed us to be around for a very long time,
And you know what it is? God's grace sublime.

Dorothell Muldrow

DEPARTING POEM FOR THE CLASS OF '66
50th Class Reunion

I'm so glad we had fun, it was such a delight,
With such elegance in place, made everything so right.
We are going back home now, with memories in mind,
Of classmates and the beautiful occasion, that we left behind.

Thank you, Judy, for a job well done,
We all worked hard, and we had some fun.
Your officers and other classmates, helped in some way,
In making sure all things were done to meet our special day.

God covered us, just like He said He would,
With the prayers we interceded for, He so willed and could.
Thanks goes to our special guest that joined us in our travel,
and those that traveled the distance to be with us,
(Gloria, Sheila, Elaine, Betty, and Evelyn).
If there were others I missed, thank you for just being on the bus.

Thank you to our bus driver Mr. Isaac and wife Ethel,
For getting us safely around,
Guarding our every footstep as we stepped on ground.
God bless your business Mr. Isaac, as you go along,
Keep God in your business, and your business will keep strong.

Farewell dear classmates, I will never forget this 50th year,
We will always and forever reminisce on the memories so dear.
Melvin took great pictures, we were so proud to have him there,
The great memories in those pictures, will keep our heart so near.

A POEM FOR ARCOLA

Arcola, I did this poem for you to say,
That I will miss you on your day, Wednesday.
I look forward seeing you in the early morn,
To hear a word from you, that God adorn.

You're sitting in your corner chair, when I make entrance through your door;
To greet me and say "Good morning," and to see a new day once more.

I met your son Marshall, as he keeps moving along;
God granted him a miracle, for when he is weak, He is also strong.
2 Cor. 12:10
I met your brother R.L., when he came happily by;
He likes your *banana pudding*, and that's the reason why.

It was good to see some of your family tree;
And the bonding relationship is very good to see.
Family is important, as each one comes by,
To give a hug, or kiss, or even a loving cry.

Your love for your kitty cats, as they cry to be fed;
The one with the fuzzy tail is my choice instead.
They are very good companions, as they accompany you;
The language between them is also comforting too.

I like your backyard and the porch, with its adoring hue;
Your plants, your vines, your special touch, makes such a nice view.
Mrs. Arcola, it's certainly nice knowing you;
And to have met your needs, with the things you had me do.

You are a courageous lady, with magnificent years;

Dorothell Muldrow

Besides, who can say about the years ahead;
My God will grant you strength and stride.
Bless you Mrs. Arcola, and in all the things you do,
God's got His arms all around you and will take good care of you.

On a Personal Note – Specialized Poetry for All Occasions

Section Seven

Get Well

Dorothell Muldrow

A GET WELL POEM FOR NANCY

Nancy, a get-well wish has been extended to you,
We truly miss seeing your face and smile too.
You were missing each day from the store,
But your sister Anne kept things nicely for sure.

God kept you in his loving care, and He got you back home,
That was my prayer for you, for strength to overcome.
Being in the hospital, didn't give you much rest,
But it gave you the opportunity to be at your best.
Of course, all the tests.

You passed the test Nancy, because you came home,
Please take care of yourself, we like having you around doing the norm.
Your sister was so kind, to help out in your place,
She was able to find many things, and she kept up the pace.
It gets busy sometimes, which is very good,
It lets you know that you have what people need, and that's understood.

Just a get well wish to keep you lifted up,
Try some of your apple cider in your special cup.
Try pineapple juice too, it seems to be good,
It's good for me, it often betters my mood. My digestive system…that is *smile*.

We like having you around,
With your feet back on the ground.
What a beautiful sound, no longer homebound.

God granted you more time,
And that is truly grace sublime.

I hope you are being strengthened as you meet each day,
Limit some things, get them out the way.
Let them go! I pray.

    God's Grace is sufficient.

Dorothell Muldrow

A POEM FOR ALPHONSO AND THEOLA OF GOD'S FATE

Al and Theola, this poem is for you, because I know what you both been through.
You are an example, of the vows you took,
Through "sickness and in health," and other things by the book.

You met the appointments, by a strict command,
Courageously enduring, the plight God planned.
Your faith and belief, and to say we must,
Travel the distance, and that was a plus.

You traveled that distance, at your very best,
And followed up the appointments, and also the test.
You fulfilled the requirements, of the things you were asked,
Following every procedure, that weren't too much a task.

This has proved to you both, that God can do all things,
By meeting those unexpected plans, that life often brings.
You received a spiritual gift, that gave you life anew,
Our God can do the impossible, with blessings and a cure.

I observed the commitment, and perseverance you showed,
Of sticking to it, even when the valley was low.
You trusted God, and His healing touch,
Knowing it was His will, and Him loving you so much.

Brother and sister-in-law, you have won this extraordinary fight,
With God's Holy Spirit, which makes all things right.

Blessings and love to you both.

A POEM FOR EDELL – A LADY OF FAITH

A poem for you Edell, because of your plight of the inevitable,
You believed by faith, and it turned out incredible.
Our Supernatural God stepped in I'm sure,
He turned things around and made things better once more.

I like the way God does things, especially when you believe,
He changes those tough situations, and the problem He does relieve.
I know where you've been, and I see you now,
I don't know everything, but I see God's Grace somehow.

This is to encourage you on the path where God is in lead,
Don't let nothing or nobody interfere, because God will continue to give you what you need.
Your grands are so lovely, and you take such good care of them,
God kept you around so you can groom them, just like him.

Your family and your sisters are very close knit,
In supporting each other, and you never quit.
It is so unique, how you all connect,
That's what God does, when you let Him direct.

It is not easy all the time, and sometimes you may not feel so good,
Remember, God promise never to forsake you, He's feeding you with His food.
Keep up your supporting, be prayerful in every way,
God is keeping you for a purpose, just smile, you will see it one day.

Dorothell Muldrow

A POEM FOR MARTHA ANN – COURAGEOUS LADY OF CHOICE

Ann, is what most people call you, and this poem is for you,
Of admiration of a true warrior, combating the journey you've been through.
I know you've seen God's glory, through your experiences and then some,
All the burdens and pain you endured, you still knew where your help came from.
Sometimes when I see you Ann, I get teary-eyed and I nod,
You have scar prints over your body, witnessing that you know God.
To see you back ushering, at one time seemed impossible,
 But God ushered you right back to your post called, "INCREDIBLE."
Now that is a testimony that will last throughout your lifetime,
God did not do this by chance, it is proof of His love sublime.
It took courage and it took might,
But most of all, it took you in this fight.
You are a courageous lady, because you battled it and you are still here,
Not looking like what you've been through, only God could meet you there.
I know prayer is the answer for the world today,
Above Him there's no other, Jesus is the way.
Ann, I truly enjoyed writing these words, also to encourage you too,
This is a gift God gave me through my journey I've been through.
Oh yes, I have a story, I get tears of joy as I think of it,
God refined me through that experience, I'm grateful, I'm thankful of every bit.
Keep on looking up Ann, because God has been with you,
God does not make mistakes, so be a witness for Him too.

BETSY'S PLIGHT
Betsy Bird with much love and get well wishes.

Oh what glory! Oh what joy! To be a vessel of our God.
To be made ready for a journey; To walk the path as Jesus trod.

What glory we've embraced; To see this miraculous deed,
No one but our God can do this, to such a special seed.

It has been a journey; And His Glory is still foreseen,
As He amends and restores and preserves you from within.

I know my God is great; His wonders never cease,
I've seen too many things he's done, in leaps, in bounds, and increase.

Betsy, you know who God is; You have seen what He can do,
He did an awesome exchange of life…with His deliverance and healing for you.

This plight has not been easy; nor with the things which have been done, but the fervent prayers of the righteous availed much; And victory has been won!

Dorothell Muldrow

A POEM FOR MURRAY
One of Strength and Vigor
for Murray Jordan for encouragement during these times. The Caring Hearts of The FloWriters' Guild

Hello Murray, it's good to see you back at the writers' table,
The bed couldn't keep you down, and it's good that you are able;
To be with us once more, only God can do that,
Those stages can only be a number, because God wears the hat.

We don't know God's plans for you,
But His will so desires, what will be the best thing to do.
You know the man, and I feel you know Him very well,
And He's the only one that can tell.
You will take one step, each moment, and each day, at a time.
You can do these things, it won't cost you one dime.

I like your wit, it brings much fun,
So good to have you around the table, as normal, we get it done.
Meantime, Murray, we are praying for you,
For continued strength and vigor, while God's will comes through.

On a Personal Note – Specialized Poetry for All Occasions

Section Eight

Enjoyable Road Trips

Dorothell Muldrow

THE ENJOYABLE ROAD TRIP

In June of 2011, my husband Reuben and I, and two friends: E.B. and Doris Burroughs went on a road trip together.
We were determined to make this trip, in spite of any inclement weather.
We decided to take our time, two weeks we say,
We will stop to visit with family and friends along the way.

We started from South Carolina up the northeastern coast,
We crossed many cities and structures, so much to see, so much to boast.
We stopped into a few places, to sleep and to rest,
But when we got to Barnegat, New Jersey, now that was one of the best.

We visited with family of our traveling friends; we spent three nights there,
So much hospitality, it was more than we could bear.
It made us felt to give back, but they said, "Don't you dare."

We left there feeling hearty, moving on up the northeastern coast,
No place in particular, just enjoying it the most.
We brushed by parts of New York, also Connecticut, then Mt. Vernon,
Then we stopped in Ontario, NY, of course to visit Allean and Leon.

Oh what a nice visit with them both and with their family,
Great fellowship, food and fun, and were hosted so nicely.
Thank you, Leon, for your sister Eunice for putting us up for three nights,
She and her husband did not mind, we were considerate and conserved the lights.

The hospitality was most gracious, and we certainly had fun,
Seeing the ducks swimming on the pond, was just a beautiful addition to what had already been done.
We left there with more distance to go,
We went right on up to Canada to see the Niagara Falls flow.

Now that was a sight to see, breathtaking as I speak,
Looking at the Falls with the naked eye, our emotions were at its peak.
You can see it from the New York side, and from the Canada side too,
They gave us water ponchos, we commenced to get a view.

Canada side is what we chose,
It was so exciting to be so close, we were so near, it seemed to be right at our nose.

My, my, never seen such a creative sight before,
I truly know my God had to open that door.
How did it make me feel?
It just made me know that God is real.

We left Canada, and started traveling back,
Stopped in Rhode Island to get a little snack.
While there, I stopped into a salon, after experiencing the Falls,
I met a young lady named Donna, since then, she often calls.

She calls me her road trip friend, we connected right away,
She is now one of my dear friends in Christ, that started from that day.
Don't know if we'll get up that way again, we don't travel like that anymore,
But maybe I'll get to see her one day, before the other shore.

We left there and came past Connecticut, and back to New York – The Bronx,
Spent some time with my husband's sisters, now in that busy city,

there were many car honks.
The visit was nice, we spent a day and night,
Then traveled to a Family Reunion, with the family last name "White."

This reunion was connected with family that lived in Maryland and Washington, DC,
So we had a large cut out paper doll of President Obama as our visible guest to see.
This was our last visiting stop, so we gave hugs and farewells to all,
We certainly won't forget this awesome road trip, we surely had a ball.

We had a grand time wherever we were, with food, fun, and fellowship,
Made our way back to South Carolina, and we can truly say, "We had an enjoyable road trip."

On a Personal Note – Specialized Poetry for All Occasions

Section Nine

Descriptive Poetry

A POEM TO BARBARA

It is a pleasure to do a poem for you of things I observe,
Even those things unknowingly to you, that's been in reserve.
Just to let you know, while observing you,
I glimpse your growing garden, I see you have a green thumb too.
You said you didn't really know very much about doing this,
You certainly surprised me, there's not very much you've missed.

You've done very well in mapping out your life,
Pursuing more knowledge and other things without strife.
You are enjoying the ladies in your Spiritual Life Ministry,
And it is a good thing, because it is growing wonderfully.

He is guiding you into all kinds of ministry work,
No need to be concerned, because His will you cannot shirk.
When he needs you to carry out an active deed,
You will know it and go at it with His speed.

He has called you out of a whirlwind, out of the whelms of the world,
To teach our sisters and brothers of the things they never heard.
God knows of his choosing, He makes no mistakes,
Just let Him stir you and see what difference it makes.

Keep an eye out, he's watching you,
He will comfort and strengthen you on this journey too.
He has embraced you with a special view,
That will win some souls, and to comfort those dismayed and blue.

The knowledge that you are seeking, oh, it will be fine,

On a Personal Note – Specialized Poetry for All Occasions

God will order your steps, and keep you in line.
He knows what we all need, when we are at a lost,
He will gird up your loins, and you will go, no matter the cost.

I will end this poem, to say God loves you,
Please be encouraged, He will see you through.

Dorothell Muldrow

A POEM FOR BETTY – A FRIEND AND SISTER IN CHRIST

A poem for you Betty Davis, to express the person I see in you,
Let's say you are a confident friend and have proved yourself to be true.
Betty, you've lived by the book, and have taught very well,
You've taught how to hang on in there, after gone through trials and tests, you will excel.

You had your babies, one then twins,
Which are all grownup now and holding their own ends.
You raised them to be independent, and you gave them a good start,
Now they are living a life of their own, remembering to never forget me not.

Not forgetting how they were raised,
Not forgetting who is their guide,
Not forgetting to respect themselves;
But most of all, keeping God's word inside.

Betty you give so much care to the children, at the childcare every day,
You teach discipline and manners, with much correction directed their way.
They leave a better person, coming from the old school rule,
There's not much of that anymore, teaching with the right tool.

But that's alright, Jesus says, "When you do it to the least of them, you did it unto me,"
Just keep on doing what you know is right, you will be blessed abundantly.

Betty, it was nice writing a few things of observation that I see,
You haven't changed at all and have been a blessing indeed to me.

A POEM FOR BEULAH
An Usher and Servant of Choice

Beulah, it fell my lot to do a poem for you,
Which tells about an usher and servant so true.
I see you at your usher's post, serving as you normally would,
Meeting the needs of the people, ushering with a servant's heart as you should.

This poem is to keep you encouraged, and for you to stay focused on what is good,
Not to worry about the things that's besetting, remember, Jesus withstood.

You once said, that you felt you weren't meeting your gifted call,
But believe me, you are on the ball.
You are doing what is required of you,
Just keep on doing what you do.

Sometimes, God does not assign you very much,
He will guide you, by you staying in touch.
We say, "Lord order my steps," and we wait for our order of skill,
Then He qualifies us, and His work is fulfilled.

God has shuffled your hours, between your job and taking care of your mom,
You are doing a fine job, and you know where that's coming from.
You are so dedicated, and has been sticking to the plan,
Staying focus on God's goodness, is all you need to stand.

Our God is so awesome, and has taken good care of you,
He brought you through your sickness, with healing and blessings too.
Just keep on smiling, you have much to receive,
You will reap God's benefits, continue to trust and believe.

Dorothell Muldrow

A POEM FOR COACH WALKER
A Man of Vigor and Might

Coach Walker, this is a poem I've written for you,
You have been observed through conversation, the things you have been through.
You stand tall in stature, with much vigor and might,
You meet the challenges, also oppositions that are not always right.

Coach Walker, you certainly don't look like what you have been through,
But I've seen the before, and the after pictures of the blessings God wrought for you.
You are a miracle walking in the spirit as you must,
Because now God is using you for, "*Makn Life Mobetta,*" which has been a plus.

I thought to write about you, because it is a story to tell,
You are doing marvelous work wherever you go, and that is so swell.
So glad to say some things that will cheer you and to guide,
Pray it will inspire you to keep right on going forward, with God being by your side,

I know the kids at the school are so glad to have you around,
For coaching, encouraging, and just someone to talk to when their luck is down.
That's who you are Coach Walker, you're that person God has put in place,
To pick up and correct the many oppositions you will face.

It's good chatting about someone I've observed for a short while,
The impression that you've made in conversation, has surely shown you've gone the extra mile.
Continue your work, as God provides you hope,
Sometimes it's not easy, but stay focused, God will help you cope.

Dorothell Muldrow

HOW DOES YOUR GARDEN GROW?

This was written from a prompt at one of our FloWriters' meetings with Judy Anderson.
This is a poem of how a seed is planted in an unusual place by God.

I am a gardener and I love it very much,
I love planting seeds to see God's *Midas Touch*.
When a flower peeps through in an unusual place,
I know that God did it, and it brings a smile to my face.

I have many things that grow in my garden, and I know from whence they came,
God made the birds, and they are His little helpers in this game.
I have a Cedar Tree, a Crepe Myrtle Tree that came up on its own,
The Crepe Myrtle grew in a specific place, just where God had sown.

The Cedar Tree, I am still nurturing, to decide where to replant it,
You have to be sure about a Cedar, because when it gets big, it has to fit.
I love it when the birds bring seeds from other ground,
I look about my garden to see what can be found.

I'm so glad God helps me with my planting, and what excellent help He makes,
I just wait after planting, because he knows what it takes,
Do you know that we are also seeds, that God has planted to flourish?
Let us grow in this FloWriters' garden and let God feed and nourish.

A POEM FOR EDITH

Usher and Servant of Choice
Has gone on, but is not forgotten

Edith, it's good to give flowers while one lives,
And that is what God blessed me to do, in this poem I will give.
You've worked in your capacity, doing a servant's job,
Whenever you run into a situation while on duty,
God blesses it, and no one dares to rob.
You do not give up, you trust God to see you through,
Keeping a smile on your face, letting God's sunshine embrace you.
You shuffle your time on the home front, and you're always there for Christopher and Karen too,
You are a wonderful mother and grandma, keeping things afloat in all that you do.

You are committed to your ushering post, making sure all things are met,
Being steadfast in your serving, doing the will of the Father of no regret.

Keep your smile, and keep doing the right thing,
Giving God the glory, for all the things He'll bring.
Remember your face is the first face people will see,
Let them see God's glory in your greetings, that's the key.

It has given me great pleasure to write this poem for you,
Continue letting God use you in what you enjoy being true.

Dorothell Muldrow

A POEM FOR HENRIETTA
Incredible Lady of Choice

Henrietta, this is a poem for you, to include you among my gifts so true,
A gift of writing the things I observe, of an insight and a word they deserve.
You are incredible lady, using the gifts God gave,
You are always working in some capacity, with a measure that will save.

Whether it's a soul or whether it's something just to know,
You always put it in perspective, and it helps many to grow.
I've known you for a long time, from P.E class till now,
You certainly been able to help me, each time I'm in your presence somehow.

When I see you, I say to myself, "God has truly preserved Henrietta, and kept her energetic anew,"
I am so glad to have known you through the years, and you being a neighbor too.

I often think about the P.E. tumble, that was so difficult for me to do,
But you always had a way to help me, and I would finally make it through.
Oh, I laugh about it sometimes, how I could not do all those things,
Awkward it would always be but looking forward to what it brings.

So Henrietta you are one of God's sunflowers, that brightly shines afar,
Doing and preparing for something, and that is who you are.

I enjoyed writing this poem about you;
It's just a flower while you live,
Keep vibrant, being who you are, and more blessings God will give.

On a Personal Note – Specialized Poetry for All Occasions

A SPECIAL POEM FOR THE INSTALLATION SERVICES
for Pastor-Elect Reverend Charles Allen Moses

Charles, what an awesome occasion of installation for you,
You did not know the plans God had, and what He was going to do.
Oh what a fellowship and what a joy divine,
To have a place of order for His people in line.
You have done as God asked, and then you followed completely through,
God has granted you a work now, that He has entrusted to you.

You will climb the highest mountains,
And endure some valleys low;
Just remember God is always with you,
and will keep you in the flow.

You will declare the Word of God, and you will speak it very plain,
Because you know who Jesus is, and it won't ever be in vain.
You will walk the path where Jesus trod, you will do it as He leads,
The straight and narrow way He means, to carry out his deeds.

You will do as God expect of you, night and day you will pray,
Lord, lead me in the path of righteousness and guide me all the way.
So Charles, go forward with His word, and conduct His business as you proclaim,
Remember it's not for form or fashion, and for sure, it's not for fame.

Focus on what you are there for, to give the word so true,
The other things will fall into place, there are good people there to help you.

We wish you well, the man of God, we know you will be alright,
God's got your back on this great journey, get ready for this plight.

Dorothell Muldrow

PEN OF A READY WRITER SOCIETY

A room of wonderful, talented beings, that have a special uniqueness with astonishing vim,
It's interesting how each mind differs, I consider it a gem.
A gem is considered precious, and something to treasure too,
That's what we are **PRWS**, God's gem of a person with a view.

The writings, the poems, the books, are at their best,
We pull our thoughts together, and God does the rest.
When we do our poems and writings, to me they are a gem,
We listen to what is written, and we enjoy each of them.
We are led in the same direction to sit around the table and write,
We come up with things that are so ideal, what amazement! what we bring to light.
It amazes me of our character, we are fun-natured and comfortable to be around,
I certainly will enjoy coming to the meetings, what a good thing I've found.

Being in a room of wonderful talented beings, we each have our own special gift,
Each individual has something different to offer, the amazement of it all gives us a lift.
Just sitting around the table brings much joy and a smile,
Louise as our lead, goes the extra mile.

She emails or texts to remind us of our date,
Encouragement of what day, and time, so that we can participate.
Meeting at a designated location, where they allow us such nice space,
The atmosphere is delightful, and it proves to be the right place.

Once more, we get to read our poems and writings of this unique gem,

On a Personal Note – Specialized Poetry for All Occasions

We listen to what is written, and we enjoy each of them.
What a wonderful **Pen of a Ready Writer Society**,
Showing and telling, of the many of God's variety.
There's something about those who write; their character is pleasant indeed,
God made us to be those writers, and He always gives us what we need.

THIS LADY PERT

This Lady *Pert* is a lady of delight,
She walks in stature, in truth, and in might.
She has this kind of backbone that is wondrously made,
Where do you think it came from? None other than God's trade.

God has given her many years, with the mind to unfold…
The things of life, and the things we've been told.
What a stunning Lady *Pert*, the lady that you know,
You will see her most anywhere, as she moves to and fro.

If you get a chance to talk to her, listen to her intently,
You will find it will be inviting, as you listen sincerely.
God kept Lady *Pert*, and put her here in place,
To draw some, and to tell others, of God's grace.

God's grace is what kept her, throughout the many years,
She truly knows about God's grace, what it is, and how it cares.
Look at Lady *Pert*, can't you see it in her smile,
And how she has pressed her way the extra, extra mile.

Look at Lady *Pert*, what a winner of grace,
God did not put her here to take up empty space.
Oh what a Lady *Pert* is she,
to be created…to be all that you see.

In loving memories of Calperta Black.

SEEING OUR PASTOR THROUGH THE EYES OF HIS MINISTERS

For I am not ashamed of the gospel of Christ. For it is the power of God to Salvation for everyone who believes, for the Jew first and the Greek.
(Romans 1:16 NKJV)

Through our eyes, we clearly see,
A man of honor and dignity.
A man who's withstood this challenging plight,
A man no matter what, stayed in the fight.

Thank you for shepherding and teaching us so well,
You prepped us on what we'd needed, and encouraged us to excel.
We were always open to what you believed,
We thank you for your integrity and what we'd received.

A man of worth and integrity,
A man of deep thought of reality.
God started something in you a long time ago,
A foundation of God's word that has blessed us so.

Through the many years and experiences you've had,
They were tests of your endurance of the things He would add.
He added the trials, the tests, the highs and lows,
God did it all, even the ebbs and flows.

You would not have been qualified, if you had not experienced this plight,
Through the persevering eyes of God, He made everything alright.
Pastor Burroughs, you have declared the Gospel, and you speak it very plain,
God has a new season for you now, with something different to gain.

Dorothell Muldrow

He has added to your retiring, those quiet moments to say, "Be Still,"
He will whisper sweet peace in your ears, and say you have done my will.
We are trusting God's will for what it will be,
Great is thy faithfulness, Lord unto thee.

SUNDAY DINNER AT MRS. SARAH'S
My Story of Mrs. Sarah's Restaurant

Do you have a taste for some, "good down home cooking?" We have the most wonderful meals at Mrs. Sarah's Restaurant. We often have dinner there, but mostly on Sundays after morning service. Her food never changes, it always has the same "just right" seasonings. Her cornbread and biscuits are always tender and light in your mouth. The collards and field peas are always tasty with the cornbread or biscuits.

While I am eating my meal, I peep over at the food bar and see her stewed apples reaching out to me. I always eat them last with one of those "just-can't-eat -just-one" biscuits.

Meantime, I can hear her moving about behind the scene in the kitchen. She's getting things ready to replenish the food bar. She comes out and smiles and welcomes her guests. She is so good about showing and telling what needs to be done, and how to do it. Her youngest son and family and other family members diligently work by her side. Mrs. Sarah sticks to her same recipes and mostly the same menu. The taste and quality of her food is consistent with each visit. Let's not forget about all the tasty desserts, such as her homemade cakes and banana pudding, which are out of sight.

There may come a time when Mrs. Sarah no longer will do the cooking, however, we know that she will pass on her legacy on to the other family members or friends. Meantime, Mrs. Sarah will keep on doing what she does best, which is cooking and keeping her customers happy. Thank you, Mrs. Sarah and your staff, for such good "vittles."

Dorothell Muldrow

THE JOY OF GIVING

Joy is extreme happiness, that is not always everywhere,
You can truly find it when God is near.
Joy of giving is straight from the heart,
When you give it away, it gives you a new start.

What is joy if you can't give it away?
What is it that hinders your giving today?
Who can you choose to give some joy to?
It's not hard if Jesus is in you.

Joy is not selfish, and it is not shy,
Joy is the go between that you can't deny.
Joy is a smile when kindness is shown,
Joy is most precious to give when one is alone.

Joy of giving can reach many hearts,
Joy is an answered prayer that needs no restarts.
Joy is rendering a smile when there's nothing to smile about,
Joy can be a sweet melody that caresses the mouth.

That's what joy is to me,
It can always be an answer to the many things we see.
It's good to bring joy to someone with a kind word,
Of pleasant things they may have never heard.

There are many things that will bring on happiness,
But if joy is not attached, you will not experience true gladness.
Joy is unspeakable, and you need no quiz,
So nice to have joy, and it is of the plan that God is.

An answer to a request on joy from Mary Abraham

Meditate on these things; give yourself entirely to them, that your progress may be evident to all. **(1Timothy 4:15)**

THE PLIGHT OF DEIDRE'

To write about you Deidre' of your miraculous plight,
You would have not made it, had you not stayed in the fight.
God was right there with you every step of the way,
You could not see the results, because it was for God to say.

You have been granted a divine healing, and now you have something brand new,
You took a leap and trusted God, and now your faith is in view.
I have seen miraculously how God can build and plant,
He started a work in you a long time ago, He will complete it with no sway, nor slant.

It is so amazing in watching your progress, and now you are back in the fold,
You tapped into your healing, and there is no more hold.
Continue forward in your ministry, you're great with your assignment,
God will be your guide in this, because you are one of His investments.

God has entrusted you to do some marvelous things, of course the Children's Drama Ministry is a plus,
Continue letting God lead and guide it, it will bring glory to Him, and joy and inspiration to all of us.

And whatever you do, do it heartily as to the Lord and not to men.
(Colossians 3:23 NKJV)

THE RIGHT TOUCH CATERING

This poem is for the, "J & J Right Touch Catering,"
Always with a caring attitude, with pleasantness in your hosting.
Things are done in the "right touch order," and that's how it relates,
Very unique display, even down to the plates.

I love the daintiness, with the special frills and the perks of color,
When you look at all of this, you would think it cost a mighty great! dollar.
All one can say is, "Awe, how elegant!"
Oh how delightful with a gala look of fragrant.

I like the uniform attire, advertising who you are,
I like the unique "J & J Catering Trailer," that show you are in the right business by far.
All of the help is so excellent, and diligently working behind the scene,
Doing their part in the business, making sure everything is nice and clean.

All can be counted on for sure, making sure the serving is distributed to the count,
Keeping an eye out on the progress, being sure of the amount.
I never known you to run out of anything, there's always enough to provide,
I'm so glad about the business, and the "right touch team" is right by your side.

I know the business is blessed indeed, God has shown you favor,
Excellent menus, excellent food, with excellent flavor.
God bless your business, God bless the many miles years ahead,
Keep God in your business, and you will always receive the many smiles.

Dorothell Muldrow

EVANS FAMILY CHIROPRACTIC AND WELLNESS

A poem for you both, for your expertise,
Using your God given gift with comfort and ease.
I don't know about others, as they come through your door,
I know God has directed me to come, and that I feel for sure.

Just a note to say you both have helped me so much,
Allowing God to use your hands for the *Midas Touch*.
Thank you for making this opportunity worthwhile,
My body is shouting and shining, and it has enhanced my smile.

I cried, "Father, I stretch my hands to thee, no other help I know;"
The spirit led me to come, it not only enhances my smile,
I see myself with a different glow.
My neck was all pinched, and my body was so slow,
My muscles were all tensed, I was at a very low.
But you both took me back, and did a work on me,
Your amazing work caused the pain not to be.

Dr. Evans, you had me to turn my head left, and then to turn it right,
You had me to look up and down, I knew then that my treatment was out of sight.
I got emotional, because I knew I hadn't been able to do just that,
So happy to have been able to come, no more trouble to combat.

I pray your business treats you with much sunshine and goodness,
It will continue to flourish, remember to keep God in your business.
You don't have to shout Him, you know that He is there.
He's right there in your bosom, and that is very near.

TO GLORIA – OUR ESTEEMED MAYOR

Gloria, proud is the word I'd like to use,
The day I heard you won the seat, that was good news.

You always had the gumption to move things right along,
Things worked in your favor, and you have proven to be strong.
Strong in your ideals and ethics to make things work,
And you have proved yourself so many times, your work you do not shirk.
One thing I observe about you, is that you are down to earth and comfortable being yourself.
When God spot a person He can use, He put them in place all by Himself.
What better way to be, is to be what people can see,
Realness, stamina, selflessness, and integrity.

You have a little wit, which makes it pleasant indeed,
I smile when you are doing your speeches, because you always come up with a need.
It may be a need to be altered, or a need ready to be enforced,
You move right upon it, to make certain it follows through, of course.
That's what makes you who you are, you ran the race and you won,
The team that you work with depends upon your opinions and together, you get it done.

I write these poems about people who I spot, to spur them up,
I recognize those itty-bitty things about them, which may lead to a blessing cup.
When I complete my book of poems, I didn't want to leave you out,

Dorothell Muldrow

Because I want people to know who you are, and what you are all about.

The First Black Mayor of Darlington, SC, now that says a lot,
You've received other awards too, just being in a good spot.
A spot where someone noticed what you did,
It was something well needed, that was not hid.
A good word has much quality, it can be carried near or far,
Not only to touch a heart, but to say that's who you are.
Enough is enough, I've said so much,
Every word is the truth with a golden touch.

It's a pleasure to do this poem about you, keep up the good work,
I can see the smile on your mom's face too.

A POEM FOR CAROLYN
An Extraordinary Manager of Choice and City Council

Carolyn, you are an extraordinary manager, and you wear it very well,
You have prepped so many people for jobs to excel.
You have the character of getting the job done,
And it's done so nicely, with integrity and fun.

You've worked for Sam's for a while now, and was relocated for a short time away,
God had it in His plans of course, for you to return home one day.

For sure it came into fruition, and you came back to the manager's spot,
Of course, there have been many changes, in fact many things have changed a lot.

You met the changes like a champ, and discerned whatever was needed,
You gave ideal instructions, and in return, they were heeded.

You won the City Council, and that fit you very well too,
You wear much upon your shoulders, not only duty, but integrity and pleasantness so true.

I admire your mom, for her being such a strong tower,
She's been journeying a long, long time; only God's power.
I also admire the support she gives to all the family tree,
In return, she really enjoys the times she spends at the gatherings with glee.
Carolyn, you also do just the same,
Making extraordinary provisions is your game.
Keep up the good work Carolyn, take everything in stride,

Dorothell Muldrow

In the midst of it all, get your rest, and know in Christ you can hide.

It's not an easy task all the times, but God is there to help,
He is always so very near, and is watching your every step.
So nice to do a few words for you,
I hope you like them; this is what I had in view, so true.

Section Ten

Encouragement

BARBARA JAMES – A LIGHT FOR A DARK WORLD

That you may become blameless and harmless, children of God without fault in the midst of a crooked and perverse generation, among whom you shine as lights in the world. **(Phil. 2:15)**

You fell in my spirit today, because of the light I see in you,
This world has so much darkness, we need a light like yours to shine through.
You are one of God's light bulbs, that gives a brilliant light,
A vessel so real in character, we always know when you're in sight.

When you stand before mankind, with whatever God has prepared you to say,
You truly make it such a delight, and it makes us smile within all day.
Just a word to you, please keep up this lovely gift,
Because not only does it touch hearts, it also gives us a lift.

God bless you Barbara, for your kindness and intellect,
No one but God can design such a person, for a divine purpose, with a true Jesus effect.

A POEM FOR JOYCE & AB OF GOD'S GRACE BESTOWED

Behold, what manner of love the father has bestowed on us, that we should be called children of God! **(1 John 3:1)**

A poem for you, Joyce and Ab,
Of a few things about you I see.
Of a couple who has crossed the miles of success,
You both have succeeded and is now in a season of rest.
You are giving God the glory, of this time in your life,
To get to do some things of enjoyment, in the midst of this world's strife.
You've had great endeavors, long years instilled in each,
You counted on God's expectation, and your goal you did reach.
Continue those things you enjoy,
Reminiscing the employ,
Spending time with the grands,
Letting God be your hands.
Kindling the moments of things you did bear.
It was a journey of faith, knowing God was near.
During the ups and downs, God had your back,
As you manage in your capacity, no work became slack.
Integrity was a fact, commitment for sure,
Putting on thick skin, was well needed to endure.
It wasn't all easy, but you learned to stick to the plow,
Knowing your day of retirement would soon come, someday someway somehow.
You are active on the church front, and in the community as well,
You seem to be headed in the right direction, not a bother that I can tell.
Prayer is in place, praise and thanksgiving is also too,
Great leadership that you both are wearing;

Dorothell Muldrow

Will be a legacy to be left so true.
Keep looking up, steadfast in those things you desire,
All things that are good, God will surely inspire.

A POEM FOR MR. & MRS. GREENE
An Esteemed Couple of Stature and Strength

To you Mr. and Mrs. Greene, for the couple you are,
You have touched many lives, and kept them up to par.
God has kept you both by each other's side,
And He promised never to leave you, because in Him you can hide.

God not only kept you, but you are still touching lives,
You have certainly helped us, and so many other husbands and wives.
God kept you for the need, that not too many can fill,
It will say much for you both one day in God's book, by doing His will.
It will be displayed as a special kind,
To say this is a couple that is hard to find.
This is what I believe, and it paints a picture so true,
I will never forget you being my second-grade teacher, and you taught each of our children too.

I held on to all you taught me through our talks and encouragement;
It gave a foundation to not give up and stick to the agreement.
Life can throw a hard ball, but we take one day at a time,
We keep on trusting and believing, because God's love is sublime.

Sometimes we need help when we don't know where to turn,
He had you in place in behalf of my concern.
Things had become better, as my eyes were all off the object,
If we keep our focus on the all mighty, He will take care of the project.

So thankful for you two, although I don't get to see you as much,
Just know we appreciate you and to thank you for the *Midas Touch*.

Dorothell Muldrow

A POEM FOR KYLE SHERROD

Extraordinary Young Man

A poem for you Kyle, to say I think of you,
And to know you graduated and accomplished another grade too.
You are moving right on up, to reach that special goal,
Your last year is coming fast, each time the teacher calls the roll.

Keep striving Kyle, you are truly going to make it,
Sometimes it's not easy, but you will be worthy of every bit.
I watched you as you grew, Grandma Sadie always by your side,
No matter what she has to do, she truly enjoyed the ride.

Making sure you had the right teachers, and that is hard to come by,
Kyle just hang on in there, all these things will subside.
I'm proud of your accomplishments, and all of the things you are doing,
Keep up the good work Kyle, we are looking forward to seeing where all of this is going.

I know you have an endeavor, of something special you'd like to do,
Just don't give up on it, because your dream will come true.

A POEM FOR SHAYLAH
Junior Year Encouragement

I have written this poem for you Shaylah, to cheer you and to guide,
Your life is so important to me, just always know I'm by your side.
You have grown up to be such a young lady, in stature and with stride,
Keep your focus on things above, and not let the worldly things ride.

You are a rising Senior now, with one more year to go,
Keep going forward Shaylah, with positive things to show.
Your prom pictures are just gorgeous; you are pretty as can be,
"Pretty is, as pretty does" what you do, is what others see.

Life is not always easy; there are challenges along the way,
God wants you to make the right decisions, and not worry what one may say.
Your grandmother loves you Shaylah, and your friends and family too.
I know you will make us proud one day; we truly believe you will come through.

Dorothell Muldrow

Section Eleven

Poems

A POEM FOR ALYSSA

Thank you, Alyssa for my flower; it means so much to me,
I watched it turn its color; to a color I like to see.
A pretty rust color, so it is; and it has sentimental value so sweet,
Thank you for thinking of me Alyssa; and from this point, you've got that beat.

I hope you're doing good in school, making the most of your grade,
It will carry you far I know, when you try with effort made.
Keep being thoughtful and kind, be an example for your teachers and friends,
Please walk the talk, that you've learned; it won't be wrong, nor will it have trends.

You are now in the junior class, with another year to go,
To further your career in life, and oh so much more.
I know you'll do all that you can, because we are counting on you,
Make your parents proud Alyssa, be brave, be wise, and always be true.

Dorothell Muldrow

A POEM OF GRATEFUL THANKS TO HATTIE

A poem for you Hattie, for a woman that proves to be true,
Just to say thank you very much for all the things you do.
Most people call you Hattie, and that is what I'll call you today,
I mostly call you Mrs. Hughes, because that is comfortable to say.

You are true to yourself, true to a cause,
True in your efforts, with very little pause.
Your character is a pleasure, you embrace many who are in need,
If it's a conversation, you are ready to plant a seed.

You are a go-getter, your aim is to please,
And you have such a way, and you do it with ease.
God has given me a gift of poetry, to embrace those things I see,
It can be about the beauty in people, and what He sees them to be.

I am growing in God's wisdom, as I follow His lead,
Sometimes I get weary, but He lifts me back with heed.
He says, "Take your eyes off those things that beset you and focus on me."
That is what I do now, that is a wonderful key.

Just to thank you, through my gift of poetry,
You are a strong pillow and is doing what God has you to be.
I love writing poems, to encourage and to embrace,
It has been such a blessing, to see the looks upon each face.

I know you have many things, on your wall and upon your shelf,
You certainly didn't need an addition, of course, this is about yourself.
Love you Hattie, be happy and free,
Keep on being the person, you're cut out to be.

A POEM FOR MARGARET
An Usher of Choice

Margaret, it gives me great pleasure to write about you,
Of the things I observe, and the work that you do.
You probably ask, "Why's she writing about me?"
It's because your spirit is most pleasant, that others get to see.

I'm for one who have observed your many tasks,
Moving so intently; no one ever ask.
Over the years, I haven't seen much change,
Of how you carry out your duty, that has never been strange.

You deeply enjoy serving, with the conscience of good will,
You have never shirked your work, and never stood still.
You have a good eye out, to discover the need,
You satisfy the occurrence and does it at God's speed.

You move about so smoothly, with a pleasantness so true,
Knowing what direction, and what duty that you should do.
This comes so naturally, because it has fallen your lot,
God had already ordained it for you, it was right from the start.

I've seen many of ushers do a spectacular job too,
But you Margaret, has been such a light, not only in your serving, it also shines within you.

There's a song that says, "Brighten the corner where you are,"
And you are doing that so well,
I see a job well done Margaret, and most people can tell.

Just a lil' flower while you live, showing your battles still to be won,
Keep on persevering on your post, doing a job well done.
Continue being that light, that sits upon the hill,
Not to be hid, but in observance to God's will.
Writing poems is a gift so true,
Sharing with others of the things they do.
It is a mission and a ministry too,
To bring a little sunshine and blessings through.
Margaret, God's continued blessing to you.

A POEM OF THANKFULNESS TO KENNETH

Kenneth, we can't express how grateful we are, but we'll start by saying thank you very much,
You've blessed us so much with the CDs of music, which gives a *Midas Touch*.
You know what songs to choose, and they meet every need,
We look forward to the nice variety, and each one plants a seed.

It is so nice of you to think of us, and to do such a special deed,
Just a dose of your good music, helps to meet our daily need.
I play your CDs in the house, and we have a few in the car,
Don't want to miss out on what's next, because it keeps us up to par.

When we travel a long distance, oh how sweet the music is,
We arrive at our destination so quickly, wondering what made it such an ease.
It is the music, which is the soul's own speech,
For heights and depths, no words can reach.

This is a ministry in itself, and each song gives a praise, and they also teach.

Just a few words written in a poem to thank you ever so much,
Keep on doing what you do, putting God first, which is like putting on the *Midas Touch*.

Dorothell Muldrow

A POEM OF THANKS TO LOUISE AND LINTON

But one and the same Spirit works all these things, distributing to each one individually as He wills. **(1 Cor. 12:11)**

Thank you very much for blessing us with your musical gift.
I had no reservations at all, that it would give us a lift,
It did and what joy filled my soul,
Thank you, Louise, thank you Linton, you both are reaching the Heavenly goal.

Your music is so superior, and the rhythm and melody are so sweet,
The piano and the trumpet sound together, are so soothing to the soul, and so especially complete.
Your music will amend and restore,
It will also heal and touch broken hearts for sure.

Music is a part of atonement and assessment with our God,
He speaks to us through the lyrics, and soothe us with His *melody rod*.

God has joined together you two; let no man put asunder,
I have seen others paired together, but this one is not a wonder.

Thanking you both through my gift of writing,
It is to cheer you and to bring you good tidings.

God bless you both in all your endeavors.

A THANK YOU POEM FOR MRS. GWEN

Just to say thank you for all the work you did for us,
The invitations were just beautiful, and the bookmarks were a plus.
I am thanking you in the form of a poem,
Because it's fun for me, which is a norm.

God has given you a special gift; and it's very unique,
You certainly have helped us, and we didn't have to seek.
Thank you also for doing the thank you cards,
Didn't want to bother you anymore…
But Ingell says, "Mrs. Gwen will do them for you, her cards you will adore."

God gives us gifts and also gives talents,
Mrs. Gwen, He's given you both with His grace and balance.
So glad now, it's almost behind us,
After the cards go out, which is a must.

I certainly appreciate everyone, that made our special day come to pass,
But most of all, thanking God, for what we do for Him will last.
Mrs. Gwen, you out did yourself, with such elegance; I must say,
In the preparation and selection and getting them printed for that day.

Superb! Superb! Is all I can say,
Be Blessed! Mrs. Gwen, there are blessings coming your way.

Dorothell Muldrow

A THANK YOU POEM FOR YOU, TALAYA
for Lecture on Women's Health

Hello Talaya, just to thank you very much,
For your participation and the wonderful *Midas Touch*.
You gave great information, for our health and for our life,
You even told us how to avoid some of life's misery and strife.

I know you are making a fine doctor in your practice and your walk;
Because you did a grand presentation with your expertise and talk.
You also allowed the Holy Spirit to expel your innermost thoughts,
Now I know He has reproved you, and He will refine you of any faults.
Thank you also again for accepting this awesome challenge,
I had no doubt about it, knowing you would manage.

I thank God for the wonderful retreat we had,
Only God could direct it, and with His lead, we were glad.
Thanks for bringing a friend,
Women need this kind of trend.

We are looking forward for increase,
Maybe sixty or more at least;
See you next year, if it is God's will,
While we are waiting yielded and still.

A THANK YOU POEM TO THE NEWSOMES

And walk in love, as Christ also has loved us and given Himself for us, an offering and a sacrifice to God for a sweet-smelling aroma.

(Ephesians 5:2 NKJV)

Thank you for the invite to your lovely home,
It is just the perfect place, no other place to roam.
Thank you for the splendid meal,
But mostly the fellowship that was especially real.

The menu was very well planned,
The ribs, the turkey wings, and the beef tips were on demand.
The cabbage went fast, the corn and salad did too,
Didn't forget about the delicious yams, oh I thank you!

What's for dessert? A slice of lemon pie certainly hit the spot,
And the apple pie didn't miss a shot.
So here's the report, every bite was good,
Not very much was left over, and everyone understood.

The atmosphere was most pleasant indeed,
And the view from the window, what enchantment to take heed.
The Gazebo, the Hassock, the Landscape, and the Trail,
Such a place of serenity, and of great detail.
I looked around and I'd imagined, those areas of peaceful, "Be Still,"
To sit and to meditate on God's blessings to fulfill.

It certainly is a warm and kind dwelling place,
The love of Jesus is upon its face.
Time is of essence, and God gives us things to enjoy,

Dorothell Muldrow

The landscape is no bother, it will be done by the employ.
Relax, enjoy, and take it in stride,
Don't even be concerned about a thing, the word says, "God will provide."

Thank you for being at "Cherry Grove," for such a time as this,
Your support has been outstanding, can't be beat, and God doesn't miss.
God bless you both for being a lighted beacon,
We are enjoying you, and each and every lesson.

MR. GILES, THE MAILMAN AND SERVITOR OF CHOICE

And whatever you do, do it heartily, as to the Lord and not to men, knowing that from the Lord you will receive the reward of the inheritance, for you serve the Lord Christ.
(Colossians 3:23-24 NKJV)

You've been on our mail route for quite a while,
Delivering mail with certainty and with a smile.
You carefully place it in the box as should be,
And if it's a package to be exposed; to the back porch we can guarantee.

We appreciate your caring of critiquing your work,
For many years, each and every day, your work you did not shirk.
You have managed very well, I see Christ in your walk,
Continue that appearance on your job, your route, and your talk.

Thank you for making a difference on this route,
Doing a job well done is what it's all about.
God's people, He will specially select,
He needs those who will do things decently correct.

This is just to let you know, we appreciate what you do,
That your work has not gone unnoticed, and we appreciate you.

Dorothell Muldrow

Section Twelve

Love and Wedding

Poems

A POEM FOR YOUR WEDDING DAY

Leo and Debra, sounds like a special couple to me,
Two is a couple, and God makes three.
Only God can make this marriage last,
Always put God first and exclude all unnecessary things in the past.

Go forward in this new life, love each other without strife,
Debra love your husband, Leo love your wife.
There will be disagreements, but you will work them all out,
Remember you've made a commitment to God's promises, that's what this is all about.

Be serious in your mind about what you have done,
You took a vow, a sacred vow, and this battle will be won.
God is not mocked, what He says, it will be,
Only if you add Him to your marriage as number three.

I can't tell you what your years ahead will bring,
But I know, what you do for Christ will last, and it will be a lasting thing.
Oh what a beautiful day it was, it brought joy to your heart,
You spoke vows to each other, saying, "To death do you part."

Your marriage was blessed by Pastor Myers, anointing was in his voice,
He covered you with God's blessings, now be happy and rejoice.

Dorothell Muldrow

A POEM OF WEDDED CELEBRATION TO A LOVING COUPLE

Love will never come to an end. (I Cor. 13:8)

An answered prayer for you Ketravious and Kalesha; this day you have pledged your love,
No one but God could bring such joy and happiness, so heavenly from above.
Ketravious and Kalesha sounds like a special couple and God to your marriage as number three.

No one but God can make this marriage last,
Always put God first and exclude all unnecessary things in the past.
Go forward in your new relationship, love each other throughout your husband, and Ketravious, love your wife.

God has given you the Lord to be your comforter and guide,
He said, "To cleave to each other, I am also by your side."
The Lord will be gracious, through sickness and health,
Always remember the small things, they're sometimes better than wealth.

There will be disagreements, but you will work them out,
Remember you've made a commitment to God's promises, that's

what this is all about.

Be serious in your minds about what you have done,
You took a covenant vow, a sacred vow, and come what may, all will be won.
I can't tell you what your years ahead will bring,
But I know what you do for Christ will last, and it will be a forever thing.

What a beautiful "Wedded Celebration," what unity is in place,
And to see family and friends with smiles of joy on each face.
God bless your marriage, long life He may give,
That's about growing old together, and the many years you shall live.

Dorothell Muldrow

A WEDDING POEM FOR KERWIN & ANNETTE

Kerwin and Annette, sounds like a special couple to me,
Two is a couple, and God makes three.
No one, but God, can make this marriage last,
Always put God first and exclude all unnecessary things in the past.

Go forward in this new life, love each other without any strife,
Annette, love your husband; Kerwin, love your wife.
There will be disagreements, but you will work them out,
Remember you've made a commitment to God's promises, that's what this is all about.

Annette, I watched you grow up to be a young lady, and I am truly happy for you,
You and Kerwin will be true to each other; you sealed it with "I do."
Just remember your promise to each other, and the sacred vows you've made,
Love bears up under anything and everything, your foundation has been laid.

What a beautiful wedding day it was, to see such unity come into place,
And to have the onlookers with smiles of joy on each face.
Both your parents were so proud, to see their children join as one,
You and Kerwin will be together, some valleys low, but also some fun.
God bless your marriage, long life He will give,
That's about growing old together, many years in store you shall live.

On a Personal Note – Specialized Poetry for All Occasions

Taking your vows together were pleasant and real,
Be serious in your minds, because your vows were blessed with a seal.
God will be your keeper, be happy as you must.
Grow and mold together, remember God is just.

Dorothell Muldrow

A POEM FOR TIMOTHY & NYESHEA ON YOUR WEDDING DAY

Timothy and Nyeshea, sounds like a special couple to me,
Two is a couple, and God makes three.
Only God can make this marriage last,
Always put God first and exclude all unnecessary things in the past.

Go forward in this new life, love each other without any strife,
Nyeshea, love your husband; Timothy, love your wife.
There will be disagreements, but you will work them all out,
Remember you've made a commitment to God's promises, that's what this is all about.

Be serious in your mind about what you have done,
You took vows, sacred vows, and this battle will be won.
God is not mocked, what He says, it will be,
Only if you add Him to your marriage as number three.

I can't tell you what your years ahead will bring,
But I know what you do for Christ will last and will be a lasting thing.
Oh what a beautiful day it was, it brought joy to my heart,
When you spoke vows to each other saying, "To death do you part."

You are a special couple; God brought you two together,
Guard this union to the utmost, through the storms and through the many kinds of weather.
Talking about things of life, and what it brings,
God has your back and will correct many things.

Be happy in your union, so special, so ideal,
Pastor Burroughs and Bishop Belin consecrated your marriage with God's seal.
It was covered with heavenly blessings, so sacred, and so real.

BECAUSE WE SAID, "I DO"
Reuben & Dorothell

50 years Lord, you saw us through,
All because we said, "I Do."
We saw the "hand of God" at work,
He had a plan, we could not shirk.

Through many years of ebb and flow,
You whispered sweet peace, and said,
"I am with you as you go."
You said, "I'll cover you through the years,
There will be highs and lows, some pain and some tears."

Lord, we are standing here, witnessing our 50-year journey,
And feeling blessed; we did not need an attorney.

Lord, you've been our comforter and guide,
God gave you to us to be by our side.
Lord, you've been gracious, through sickness and health;
Thank you for the small things, they're sometimes better than wealth.

Thank you for keeping us, and dwelling within,
We could not have made it, had you not intervened.
Thank you for these 50 years, thank you for the tears,
They brought about strength of your love that cares.

Bless this special day, Lord;
Bless us with your love,
Sustain us with your power,
Heavenly Spirit, Heavenly Dove.

Dorothell Muldrow

HEAVEN SENT TWO
Cadarreus & Christina

The love that you've shared is momentous and true,
A love made in longing and is Heaven sent too.
The moments you've spent were real, and your hearts says it all,
Which drew you both together, with an unending and sacred call.

You two were meant for each other, You felt it from the start;
Did it enter your mind one moment… that you would be tying the knot?
Well, well, it has happened, and the love has struck the air;
Be good to each other forever and remember, keep God in your care.

You will be far from home now, and you will become as one;
Unity and sharing is the utmost, keep God always;
Well done! Well done!

On a Personal Note – Specialized Poetry for All Occasions

Section Thirteen

Congratulation and Graduation Poems

Dorothell Muldrow

A GRADUATION POEM FOR OUR GRANDDAUGHTER CASSIE

Cassie, it's a pleasure seeing you walk across the stage of life to a beginning of something great,
Knowing that you have many things in mind to reach and to celebrate.
You've finished your first endeavor, and you will begin a new challenge,
You will go forward with great effort, and it will be something you can manage.

You have many gifts that will embrace you, and you'll choose what is best,
This is your life aim and goal, complete it with nothing less.
Use good judgement, being wise is a good thing,
Some things you don't chance, just be patient and see what it'll bring.

There are many directions to go in this life, but be mindful in this world of change,
Take those quiet moments to talk to God, be still and let Him arrange.
With the right lead, you will avoid many mistakes,
When you do that, you will realize the uncertainty life makes.

Being young in life, somethings are unknowing to you,
But there is power and direction that God gives so true.
Have the mind of Christ to say, "I can do all things through Christ who strengthens me," *(Philippians 4:13)*
I will make this all happen, just watch me and you will see.

We love you Cassie I'Liyah, let your spirit flow,
Keep God in your spirit and you will keep the glow.

On a Personal Note – Specialized Poetry for All Occasions

A GRADUATION POEM FOR ANGELICA

I've written you this special poem Angelica, to say we're proud of you,
Congratulations! For your many accomplishments, which you marvelously came through.
You gave it your greatest shot, through your studies and steadfast zeal,
It has made this achievement worthy, and the reality of it is real.

You may not know what the future holds, and sometimes we can't always see,
But you must continue to pursue it; do not sway until it comes to be.
Press on toward your highest goal, and remember this depends upon you,
You are seeking a lifetime foundation, that will concrete this dream come true.

Angelica, you've accomplished your first endeavor and crossed one stage of life,
Be forward in your next endeavor and avoid those things that causes strife.
We will be listening out for your next accomplished goal,
And that you'll be crossing another stage of life that your future will hold.

Believe in yourself, trust the things you can do,
Your family and friends will be there to guide and support you.
Angelica, as you proceed, most of all, let God lead your way,
Aim for the right people in your path, and you'll be successful and proud one day.

Dorothell Muldrow

A GRADUATION POEM FOR CHRISTOPHER

Christopher, we are proud of you, and what you have become,
You've reached one milestone in your life, and we all know where it came from.
The Lord has blessed you mightily, with an aim to do your best,
Go forward! Be steadfast! Be very sure, and God will do the rest.

There is much support from your family, and your friends are right there too,
To congratulate you on your first endeavor; and more good work is due.
You're getting ready now, for the next chapter ahead,
You will go at it with God's zeal and won't even be afraid.

You get a little rest now, prepare yourself for this endeavor,
You're doing good, have faith in God, and you will have His favor.
When you off from home, and when consecrating on your goal,
Just know we all love you and remember what you were told.

The celebration was so wonderful; you looked great in your attire,
You are such a humble gentleman, in so many ways, to admire.
Keep God in your heart, stay focused as you go,
Think of the things that you were taught; it will lead the right path, I know.

Don't let anyone detour you, from the promise to yourself,
To achieve what is important, and what you have to invest.
God bless you Christopher H.X. Chapman; make us very proud of you,
Looking forward to seeing you on that stage, saying I made it, my dream came true.

Congratulations! Hooray! God bless.

A GRADUATION POEM OF CELEBRATION FOR DEIDRELL

Congratulations, Deidrell! For reaching your accomplished goal,
It took determination; that only God could hold.
You walked across the stage of life, with proud eyes in observance of you;
To receive your degree of achievement, that you strived so hard to do.

You did it Deidrell! With gumption so true,
It hadn't been all easy, but you made it through.
God had made provisions and has put you in place,
To start your new life's journey, you will do it with the right pace.

Remember, this is a joint effort, with God at the front,
He will provide what you need, sometimes it may be blunt.
I say that because we live in a world of good, bad, and ugly,
Take your eyes off the world's objects and focus on God only.

You have your ministry mission, that God has entrusted you with,
To touch the hearts of the young ones, who are caught up in the world myths.
Your life is being written, it will make a great book,
You are responsible for what will go in it, those challenging moments that will have you on a hook.
You kept yourself, you held up the fight,
God had you close at hand and kept that right.
Work on humility, it is a gift you will need,
It will be expressed through your messages, and many will take heed.
Congratulations once more, it's been tried and true,
Be a positive example in this new life in view.
There is much support from your family, and your friends are right there too,
This is your first endeavor, and we are counting on you.

Dorothell Muldrow

A GRADUATION POEM FOR KENDRIC DWAYNE

Delight in the Lord, and he will grant you your heart's desire.
(Ps. 37:4)

I written this special poem to say, "Congratulations and best wishes!" to you,
For your many accomplishments, which you came marvelously through.
You've crossed the first stage of life, with optimism and zeal,
Looking forward to your future's aim, knowing that life's plight is real.

This plight will be rewarding,
Just you wait and see,
Those things that friends and family have prompted you to do,
has enlightened this person you'll be.

Be a man of stature, be a man of might,
And be a man of integrity,
And gird up your loins to be ready to tackle your aim to be.
You say you want to be an actor, even to write plays,
It sounds like a great future, and it can happen only with God's ways.
Always seek God's guidance, and let Him lead the way,
Kendric, never give up, keep striving toward your goal, and it will be win-win one day.

Always be mindful, aim for the right people in your path,
Don't get cocky! Never become arrogant! Listen for the good instructions that God hath.
You'll be fine, because you have good character,

On a Personal Note – Specialized Poetry for All Occasions

Keep believing in yourself, be firm in your convictions, and that will become a true factor.

We will be listening out for the good news,
Of the next endeavor, wearing some different shoes *meaning progress successful.*

Hurrah!!

Dorothell Muldrow

A GRADUATION POEM FOR KENYETTA NICOLE

Delight in the Lord, and He will grant you your heart's desire.
(Psalm 37:4)

Kenyetta, what a day of success, and we are proud of you,
You've crossed your first stage of life, and came marvelously through,
Now you will go forward with your next endeavor of your dream,
You will pursue it step by step and will seek it with esteem.

You said you want to do real estate, that's an endeavor for sure,
Go forward with it in every way, it may just open a door.
You must trust, and try whatever you want to do,
Stay with it, keep it in mind, it will come through for you.

You may not know all what the future holds, but you must strive on to see,
Keep right on pursuing toward what you want, do not sway until it comes to be.
Do not fall for love too quickly; it could alter your plans you see,
Keep it on friendly bases, with wisdom and control, *this is the key*.
Kenyetta, whatever you do, will surely depend upon you,
Remember you are seeking a lifetime foundation that will concrete this dream come true.
You have grown up to be such a young lady with a disposition to please,
Go at life, always keep your focus on things above, and be at

ease.

You are lovely and pretty as can be,
"Pretty is, as pretty does," what you do is what others see.
Life will not always be easy, there are challenges along the way,
God wants you to make the right decisions, and answer to
Him one day.

Dorothell Muldrow

A GRADUATION POEM FOR MY GRANDDAUGHTER NAHLA

I've written you this special poem, to say we're proud of you.
You've proved yourself worthy, of the person so honored, so true.
You gave it your greatest shot, through your studies and through your zeal,
It has made this achievement worthy, and the reality of it is real.

Nahla, what you've done for yourself, is most rewarding and special indeed,
It makes the world around you, strive to do the will to succeed.
What a day of accomplishment, of this achievement and success,
I watched you upon the stage of life, seeing you at your best.

You may not know what the future holds, but you must still strive on to see,
Keep right on pursuing what you want, do not sway, until it come to be.
Do not fall for love to quickly, it could alter your plans to be,
Keep it on friendly bases, with wisdom, control, *this is the key*.

Press on toward your highest goal, and remember this depends upon you,
You're seeking a lifetime foundation, that will concrete this dream come true.

A GRADUATION POEM FOR SHAMEEK

Buy the truth, and sell it not; also wisdom, and instruction, and understanding.
(Proverbs 23:23)

Shameek, this is an occasion of celebration,
To see the finished product of your high school education.
It has not been easy, but you didn't give up,
You kept pressing forward, even when situations seemed to erupt.

I often hear you ask questions of things that you're uncertain about,
That is always good measure, so it can be worked out.
There are so many distractions, that will steer you off track,
But remember to keep your head about you, and let it not be just an act.

You have been blessed to be driving now, and it seems that you are making a good start,
Please be mindful of the road laws, and always be willing to do your part.

Go forward now to your next endeavor,
Please do the right things; and God will show you favor.
God bless you on your way up and let Him direct your ways,
He will always be with you, that's what the Bible says.

Dorothell Muldrow

A POEM FOR JACQUARD

You did amazing things plus hair, while studying your career;
Who can say where this will lead…but the Good Lord and His Seer,

We are so proud of you, and all you've thrived to be,
God ordered your steps Jacquard, and let "Divine Order" come from thee.

Be wise in your decisions; be patient in all that you do,
You can't hurry some things;
You'll have to wait till they come through.

I know you will do well, and it won't be all in vain,
Watch, wait, and pray; that's the key, and you will surely gain.

So gird up your loins Jacquard, "Fresh courage" in all your days,
God will always be with you; that is what He says.

Best Wishes to you in all your endeavors.

A GRADUATION POEM FOR SHALIK BROWN

Shalik I've written this poem to say, "Congratulations and Best Wishes to you,"
For all your many accomplishments, which you came marvelously through.

It was not all easy, this wonderful experience,
Though it was kind of like a test;
But you went forward in your efforts, and now look, you are at your best.

Oh but now, you'll have to prove yourself, in zeal and in God's might,
Rest just a little while Shalik, and get on with this plight (to pledge one's word),

This plight will be rewarding, just you wait and see,
With the things that folks have said to you;
Will enlighten this person you'll be.

Be a man of stature, be a man of might, and a man of integrity,
God's got your back, with this foundation,
So gird up, get ready, be all that you can be.

Believe in yourself, and trust the work you know that you can do,
Your family and friends will guide and support;
So get out and find your way through.

Don't get cocky! Don't get arrogant! It will not get you far in life,
Be strong, be brave, keep integrity,
It will prevent much misery and strife.

Dorothell Muldrow

Now whatever endeavors you'll proceed,
Pray God will lead you all the way;
Aim for the right people in your path,
And you'll be successful and proud one day.

On a Personal Note – Specialized Poetry for All Occasions

CHRISTINE'S HOME OF HER OWN

God has given you a home of peace and of rest,
He will also give you contentment, when you do your very best.
You have proved yourself by being responsible,
Now you can lay your head down and be very comfortable.

Your wonderful home where you will reside,
Is the beginning of new things that you will take in stride.
I know your mom and dad are proud to see,
That you are pursuing this challenge with high hopes with a guarantee.

Christine, give this your commitment, give it your all,
God knows you are trying, don't hesitate to give Him a call.
There will be ups, and there will be downs,
Just remember, God is able, no matter how bad it sounds.

Carry yourself decently, in all you thrive to do,
Attitude and character are the utmost, this will always carry you through.
Don't forget to worship, while you are away from home,
Because sometimes all the good you do, will have a tendency to roam.

Christine, I can truly say, you have impressed us mightily,
From observation I can see, you are thriving oh so nicely.
I'm so glad you are enjoying your new home,
Always keep God in all of your business, and more blessings will surely come.

Dorothell Muldrow

RUSHAUN MULDROW HOME OF HIS OWN

God has given you a home of peace and of rest,
You will work hard and give it your best.
You have proved yourself by being responsible,
Now you can lay your head down on your own and be very comfortable.

Your wonderful home is on this special avenue,
It will be permanent because we are counting on you.
I know your mom is smiling down, to see you are making a life for yourself,
You are pursuing this challenge, and not depending on what's left.

Carry yourself decently in all you thrive to do,
Attitude and character are the utmost, this will always carry you through.
Don't forget to worship, while you are away from home,
Because all the good you do, sometimes have a tendency to roam.

Rushaun, I can truly say; you have impressed us mightily,
From my observation, you are thriving so nicely.
I am so glad to have joined this celebration of your new wonderful home,
Always keep God in your business, and more blessings will surely come.

Blessings to you, Rushaun.

A HOUSE WARMING POEM FOR DEBRA HUDSON

God gave you this home of peace and of rest,
He will give you contentment when you do your very best.
Give it your commitment, make your ends meet,
Lay your head on your pillow knowing God is mighty sweet.

Let love be your first goal, as you go in and out,
Let God be the head of your home, that's what God's love is all about.
Making the right decisions, and let God have it all,
God knows you are trying, just give Him a call.

Sometimes there will be ups, and sometimes you will meet some downs,
Just remember that God is able, no matter how bad it sounds.
Gird up your loins, face each day with a smile,
Do whatever is necessary, God will be your speed, and always will be your mile.

"Dee Dee," enjoy your new home with blessings.

Dorothell Muldrow

A GRADUATION POEM FOR NICHOLAS

We are fellow-workers in God's service; and you are God's garden. Or again, you are God's building. **(1 Cor. 3:9)**

This poem has been written to wish you well today,
You've finished your endeavor and great work is on the way.
God granted you much success and much esteem,
To go out in the world today to do what God has deemed.

Nicholas LeVar, we are proud of you, for reaching this accomplished goal,
You persevered and studied hard for God's word to be foretold.
God has granted you many blessings, through compassion and steadfast zeal,
You've proved yourself in many ways, by dedication and commitment so real.

Very few Sundays you've missed, Granddad Preacher taught you well,
Keep on doing what you do at best; God's light will show and tell.
You play your drums in the corner, and never miss a beat,
Now God's got an added job for you; to all the people you'll meet.

We will hear inspired words from you, straight from Heaven itself,
I hope to receive your many gifts of teachings (the book club), to put upon my shelf.
Your dedication has paid off you know, as you traveled to and fro,
God had His eyes upon you Nicholas, granting you safety as you go.

You have been entrusted to be a vessel for the Lord,
Take heed to all it's worth Nicholas and be on one accord.

A POEM FOR GEORGE

Wooo-hoo!!! Indeed, you got the job with tons of ideas and fun to come;
God saw your work and others did too, what a blessing, what favor, and then some.

So gird up your loins, get ready for the dive;
Don't think along fame and fortune,
God's Glory is what you thrive.

I knew it was coming George,
God has put it into place;
In a position that has great potential,
And with a smooth pace.

Go for it! Do it! As you would do unto Him;
I grant you, as you flourish,
You will know that your reward is not with them.

Heaven is your goal. Give God all the Glory.

We are happy for you.

Dorothell Muldrow

A CONGRATULATION POEM FOR REV. ANTWAUN RICHARDSON

The Faithful Will Abound with Blessing. **(Proverbs 28:20 NIV)**

Antwaun, this is a poem of extreme gladness for you,
You have accomplished your work of and have brought blessings back so true.
You always have declared the Word, and now it has a *Midas Touch*,
Another one of the new things God is doing, and He thanks you very much.

I know that those who will hear, will be inspired by the words you've been taught,
To make ready His people who are lost and distraught.
Time is winding up, it's closer now it seems to be,
God is always open to change hearts, He's ready to rescue as we can see.

I like when the word is brought plainly, with understanding and clarity,
You will do well with that, I have no doubt that it will be done mightily.
I remember when you were with the "Praise Ministry," and you dramatized the song, "I Prayed About It,"
You didn't know you were opening a door for yourself, on answered prayer for the pulpit.

That's the way God is, the mysteries of His ways,
He knows our every being, since the "Ancient of Days."
God bless you Antwaun, as you bring the Word,
Declare it! Proclaim it! But most of all, touch those who have never heard.

Antwaun, I have no doubt about it, God has a plan in store for you,
Listen to His voice in quiet time;

On a Personal Note – Specialized Poetry for All Occasions

He will surely guide you on what to do.
These are my wishes for you, to bring glad tidings to God's people,
Let it be in season and out of season;
Stand fast! God will guard you and be your keeper.

Dorothell Muldrow

Section Fourteen
Initial Sermon

A POEM FOR EMANUEL JAMES DOBSON'S INITIAL SERMON

Run the great race of faith and take hold of eternal life for to this you were called, when you confess your faith nobly before many witnesses.
(1 Timothy 6:12)

Emanuel, you have declared the Word of God, and you speak it very plain,
You know who Jesus is, and you know it's not in vain.
You will climb the highest mountain, with His word you will proclaim,
It is not for form or fashion, and no it's not for fame.

You will walk the path where Jesus trod, you will do it as He leads,
The straight and narrow way He means, to carry out His deeds.
You will do as God expect of you, night and day you will pray…
"Lord, lead me in the path of righteousness, and guide me all the way."

"Lord, keep me every day I pray, bless our marriage union, and beautiful family as we grow,"
"Bond us lord forever true, in unity, in spirit, here below."
"Bless my ministry Lord, and guide my every step,
It is you Lord that will keep me humble, and I can always count on your help."

Blessings to you, Minister Dobson.

Dorothell Muldrow

ACKNOWLEDGMENTS

First of all, I want to thank Mrs. Barb Thayer for teaching me computer skills on Tuesdays and on how to use the computer properly. We began that journey in 2011. Had it not been for her help, I would still be hopelessly computer-illiterate. The time she spent helped me to advance in computer knowledge. My confidence grew, and I started writing a lot more.

The gift of writing is now being put on a higher level, and it's all because of the lessons taught by Mrs. Thayer. I can work putting things together more proficiently. God started a work in me of writing lyrics for songs and poetry in 2008. I still have a lot to learn, but as I write, knowledge and memory will come. God knew it would benefit me to put things in the proper perspective, and He knew exactly who to send to help me.

I want to appreciate Mrs. Carolyn Addison. She teaches English for the Morris College Extension for Christian Education where I attended for 5 years. I was one of her students. She taught me so much with my writing style and skills. I laugh now at some of the things I had written, thinking my writings were so right, but they were so wrong. I am still far from perfect as a writer and you still may find errors, but I do love writing. I can depend on Mrs. Addison for setting me straight and correcting my errors. I didn't know at the time that God was constructing and building me for something major that I would be doing later in life that would greatly impact others.

I would also like to thank The FloWriters' Group, which is a group I joined through the advice of a classmate, once she discovered I was a writer. The FloWriters' Group is near my hometown. We would sit around the table twice a month, each reading their own work while others gave help through opinions, critiques, and corrections. We also sat around the table and worked on prompts for enjoyment.

On a Personal Note – Specialized Poetry for All Occasions

I acknowledge and appreciate Antoinette Free, a family member who, as well, shared her time helping me with some of the computer skills. God is an awesome God.

If it were not for the skill of Roosevelt Davis, I might not have gotten my work converted from the old computer system to the new for the publishing of my first book!

In retrospect, I got started in this direction and didn't know what was happening to me nor did I know what to do. I was so awestruck in so many ways, but I knew to be still and let God order my steps; knowing sooner or later, His divine direction would be clear. I continued jotting down what God would give me, tucking it away until the appointed time. Suddenly, He let me reconnect with a young lady named Louise Smith. I hadn't seen her in many years. We met at a church appreciation program where I was also attending. She is a musically talented person and has many other God-given gifts. I have always admired her music and if I heard she would be in concert or whatever musical treat she would be a part of, I would make every effort to be a part of the experience. We briefly chatted, and I asked her about some of her music to add to my music library. She took my address, and in a short while I received the music in the mail. In return, I sent her a poetic, thank-you note. She seemed to be genuinely blown away and called me the day she read it. I knew she and her spouse were Recording Artists, but I further learned she's an Author, Speaker, and has a book publishing company. I said to myself, "Look at God."

God will give the push needed in the right direction at the right time. Won't God do it? Mrs. Smith told me I have a gift and need to give birth to the dream. When she heard me perform my poetic and lyrical work, she liked it. Now here we are with my first published work, "On a Personal Note: Specialized Poetry for all Occasions. Hurrah, for Kingdom Builders Publications! I'm on my way!

Dorothell Muldrow

ABOUT THE AUTHOR

Dorothell Helena White-Muldrow, born in Brooklyn, NY to the parents of James and Helen Dorothell White. As a young child, she and her brother moved south to live with their grandparents.

She is married to Reuben Muldrow and to that union there are four children: Lisa, Marquis, Ingell, and Anthony. They have a rich legacy of 11 grandchildren.

Dorothell's hobbies include sewing and flower gardening. In her spare time, she like visiting garden nurseries, Bible bookstores, and antique shops. These things brighten her day.

God endowed Dorothell with something extraordinary. Her personal ministry inspires, encourages, heals, and brings joy. She shares that gift with words through songwriting, poetry, a little baking, and foliage giving.

Dot, as she is affectionately called by close friends and family, watched her writings emerge on the scene in the early 2000's. She's been writing about 17 years. Her first writing was revealed through a dream about her pastor's wife who taught her the lyrics of a song with title and music to, "That's Love, God's Love." Out of the dream came five stanzas she vividly heard, saw, and committed to memory only by God's divine help. Through this song, the message was impactful for others.

The song in the dream was like a nursery rhyme where God beckoned her to come, sit, and hear Him as a child, which was the beginning of a beautiful gift of writing songs and poetry.

The amazing thing is I know that it is God, and I believe and trust Him with all of me,

To do and write what the spirit gives me to see.

This beautiful gift of poetry will be a legacy,

To enhance, to enjoy, to embrace, and to encourage what I see in others to be.

I let God order my steps with this,

He holds my hand, and I know He's in the midst.

I give all honor, glory, and praise to God this day,

For using me to bring about a work in such a unique way.

www.ingramcontent.com/pod-product-compliance
Lightning Source LLC
Chambersburg PA
CBHW062026290426
44108CB00025B/2794